NEW DIRECTIONS IN ECONOMIC AND SOCIAL HISTORY

New Directions in Economic and Social History

Edited by
Anne Digby
and
Charles Feinstein

LYCEUM
BOOKS, INC.

224 S. Michigan Ave.
Chicago, IL 60604

First published 1989

Published in Great Britain by
MACMILLAN EDUCATION LTD
Houndmills, Basingstoke, Hampshire RG21 2XS
and London

This U.S. edition published by
LYCEUM BOOKS, INC.
224 S. Michigan Avenue
Chicago, Illinois 60604

Printed in Hong Kong

ISBN 0–925065–25–0

Contents

Figures

Illustrations

Tables

Maps

Introduction

ANNE DIGBY, CHARLES FEINSTEIN

This volume aims to bring to a wider audience some of the important new interpretations made in recent years by those working in the field of economic and social history. Increasing specialisation in subject-matter, and a growing emphasis on quantification in methodology, have meant that many important advances in this field have not been accessible to the general reader. To help overcome this the Economic History Society decided to sponsor a publication specifically designed to enable the leading specialists in the subject to present the results of their latest research to a more extensive readership. All the chapters in this volume were originally commissioned for the journal, *ReFRESH*, (*Recent Findings of Research in Economic and Social History*). *ReFRESH* set out to show that complex arguments could be made accessible in simple stages through the use of a clearly structured text and explanations of technical vocabulary in special glossaries. Authors were asked to use plentiful tables, figures, illustrations and maps to clarify the main points of the argument, and to present information in a variety of mutually reinforcing ways.

ReFRESH was initially intended primarily for teachers, but the response to the first few years of publication indicated that many others, including pupils and college undergraduates, also found the material extremely helpful. It was therefore decided that it would be worthwhile to make the articles available to a wider audience. In this volume leading scholars discuss new answers to old problems, for example, the reasons for the rapid growth of population in the late eighteenth century, the effect of industrialisation on the standard of living, the results of enclosures, and the nature of Chartism. The authors show how new evidence from archival sources, new methods of analysis and new approaches have helped to change our understanding of these major historical issues.

They also take care to relate their current findings to older, more familiar views of the same subject.

What are some of the main features of these new directions in economic and social history which are surveyed here? One very obvious characteristic of much new work is an emphasis on gradualist interpretations. Instead of the dramatic changes which featured in earlier work, with its emphasis on 'revolutions' in industry or agriculture, there is now an enhanced appreciation of the long-term nature of economic growth and change. For example, Crafts decisively rejects the view of developments in the 'classic' period of the industrial revolution from 1780 to 1830 as a dramatic 'take-off', and replaces this with a picture of steady economic growth sustained over a long period. In a very different field, Middleton's discussion of the rise and fall of the managed economy in the twentieth century also suggests that a longer view must be taken of the Keynesian revolution in the light of the new evidence now available. This has altered the historian's judgement on the origins of the problems encountered in making the transition to a new role for the government in economic policy-making, the speed with which Keynesian ideas were accepted, and the impact they had on the economy. Similarly, Overton's discussion of successive agricultural revolutions stresses how crucial the definition of the *concept*, as well as the historical *record*, is to a satisfactory assessment of the place and character of innovation.

A related question which frequently emerges when the contours of economic and social history are redrawn is whether change or continuity is the more prominent feature of historical development. This issue is central to several chapters – as in discussions of topics as varied as Domesday Book, the welfare state, or women in modern Britain. Recent interpretations have tended to emphasise continuities; underlying structures that remain under changing forms. An example of this is Harvey's analysis of Domesday Book, which she sees as a welding together of Anglo-Saxon practices and Norman feudal interests. What is also notable here, as in other recent work in social history, is a widening of the area of vision; a better appreciation of the ways in which historical context can either interact with what had hitherto been seen as the central

2

event or subject, or alter one's evaluation of it. In her assessment of the growth of the welfare state, for instance, Thane reminds us of the significant space that remained for voluntary action and self-help, despite an increase in collectivist provision. The roles of different forms of welfare may thus have grown side by side, not as substitutes for each other. She also emphasises the limited capacity of welfare measures to effect social change.

Another theme which emerges from these studies is that new work that changes our perception of one aspect of the economic past may lead to, or be accompanied by, a different perspective in a related area. Given that industrialisation is now seen as a much more protracted and diffuse process than formerly, Hopkins argues that imperialist impulses cannot be understood without placing much more emphasis on the long term. And instead of linking nineteenth-century British imperialism to industrialisation – in the traditional sense of industry and empire – he suggests that less emphasis should be placed on manufactures and more on the growth of finance and services. Wrigley and Schofield's mould-breaking work on demographic changes in early modern Britain, with its focus on the argument that marriage was the key variable in population growth, has also led to fresh insights into economic growth and standards of living during the 'long' eighteenth century. Wrigley suggests that since marriage behaviour was sensitive to economic circumstances, severe population pressure on resources could be avoided by deferring marriage. People in early modern England could thus enjoy relatively high incomes and good standards of living. In reviewing standards of living achieved during and after industrialisation, Floud also brings new data – this time on height – to illuminate an old debate. He shows that changes in height reflect changes in nutrition and thus provide a good guide to several important components of living standards. On this basis he concludes that his data provide additional evidence on deprivation suffered by the working class in the early nineteenth century and, more speculatively, an indication of the large extent of unemployment towards the end of the century.

In some other work in social history what has produced new

findings is a different angle of vision from which to view subjects that are familiar in general outline. In the reviews in this volume of recent work on Chartism, Domesday Book, or the aristocracy of labour, the fresh visibility of women is an illustration of this process at work. In each case women had previously been largely overlooked, whereas they are now seen to have played significant roles. Lewis's extended discussion of women and society since 1870 indicates that discovering historical data on women – although sometimes posing difficulties – is relatively straightforward compared to the problems that arise when this information is interpreted. Successive generations of feminists, for instance, have had very different ideas as to what constituted 'progress' in women's lives.

The eye of the beholder is obviously crucial to historical interpretation; individual biases of historians have played a significant role in creating our vision of the past. Several chapters in this volume exemplify the way in which an earlier 'black and white' image of events – in which economic gains were contrasted with social losses – has become less clear-cut in recent work. The traditional view saw the Highland Clearances in terms of poverty resulting from dispossession. By contrast, Devine's analysis of recent work substitutes a more complex interpretation in which destitution is seen to have been widespread even before population displacement led to a further deterioration in standards of living. His assessment of the variety in economic conditions within the highlands and, leading from this, his conclusion that the clearances had a differential impact, is parallelled by Turner's judgement on the economic and social consequences of parliamentary enclosure. Turner considers that the debate over the relative economic efficiencies of open-field against enclosed farming is as yet unresolved and that, in social terms, enclosure 'lubricated' the emergence of a rural proletariat but was not its sole or main cause, as some earlier writers had argued.

However, it would be wrong to assume that the outspoken conclusions of earlier historians, typified by the socially-concerned and polemical style of the Hammonds, should always be dismissed. Many of the issues raised in this earlier, darker interpretation of the effects of urbanisation and industrialisation continue to preoccupy modern writers. Moreover, reinvestigations following from discovery of new evidence or the deployment of more sophisticated techniques may serve only to confirm earlier conclusions. While this must be recognised it is true that much new work has challenged, modified or overturned previously accepted opinions. The fires of controversy are kept well stoked, and one cause of this is the ideological position, whether implicit or explicit, adopted by the historian. This is particularly noticeable in labour history – as Royle's survey of the changing interpretations of Chartism reveals. He argues that an economic interpretation of Chartism can no longer be regarded as adequate and that there is now a greater appreciation of its political dimension. The political element in interpretations of the economic gains achieved by the 'labour aristocracy' is also revealed in Morris's account. He reviews the competing hypotheses of bribery by employers versus collaboration by a working-class élite, but suggests instead that the privileged economic position of this group of workers was accounted for both by their bargaining strength and their independent cultural values. The transformation during the nineteenth century of cultural values in the education and recreation of the working class as a whole is central to Thompson's close scrutiny of the much used – and abused – concept of social control. In addition, he draws attention to the way in which historians have borrowed concepts, terminology or techniques from other disciplines to refurbish their tool-bags.

The expansion of this tool-bag in recent years has had very obvious gains. The chapter on population reveals, for example, how technical and data-deficiency problems have been overcome both by the methods of family reconstitution and back-projection, and by the use of parish registers. This has helped to settle very longstanding disagreements over the relative importance of trends in fertility and mortality. All chapters emphasise this view of economic and social history as a subject concerned with continuing debate rather than with cut-and-dried facts. Authors indicate the ways in which research and discussion might develop profitably in the future. Only a few of the areas in which exciting new work is being pursued are covered in this first volume of *New Direc-*

tions in Economic and Social History. More topics are planned to appear in further issues of *ReFRESH*; subscription details of this journal can be obtained from the editors at the Department of Economics in the University of York. Later, the articles will appear in successors to this volume.

I Agriculture

1 Agricultural Revolution? England, 1540–1850

M. OVERTON

The story of an agricultural revolution introduced by aristocratic heroes in the century after 1750 has proved a surprisingly enduring myth. Like early accounts of the industrial revolution it is a late Victorian tale that captured the popular imagination with its emphasis on particular innovations (turnips, the Norfolk four-course rotation, and mechanical gadgets such as the seed drill), and the Great Men associated with them ('Turnip' Townshend, Coke of Holkham, and Jethro Tull). Although subsequent research in agrarian history has shown this traditional account to be a grossly misleading caricature there is no consensus among agricultural historians about an alternative view of the nature or the timing of a decisive transformation in agriculture.

AGRICULTURAL REVOLUTIONS

The phrase 'agricultural revolution' is now used to refer to a multitude of events and processes taking place at some point during the three centuries after 1550. Using work published in the 1960s it is possible to identify three distinct periods during which it has been claimed that an 'agricultural revolution' took place. This essay will outline each of these in turn, and then comment on them in the light of some of the most recent research in agrarian history. This research shows that the process of agricultural change is too continuous and too varied to enable any one episode in a long history of development to be identified as *the* agricultural revolution. The essay also

9

includes a brief discussion of the *concept* of an 'agricultural revolution' since the existence of such a phenomenon is not something that can be determined by examining the facts of history alone.

PERIOD 1: 1750–1850

Over the years research has diminished the reputations of the 'Great Men'. It has been shown that 'Turnip' Townshend was a boy when turnips were first grown on his estate and Jethro Tull was something of a crank and not the first person to invent a seed drill. Coke of Holkham was a great publicist (especially of his own achievements) but some of the farming practices he encouraged (such as the employment of the Norfolk four-course rotation in unsuitable conditions) may have been positively harmful. More generally it is acknowledged that the traditional picture of a sudden and rapid transformation in the eighteenth century is mistaken, and that some improvements had long antecedents. Nevertheless a revisionist view of the traditional story, which owed much to the work of G. E. Mingay, still firmly located an agricultural revolution in the century after 1750. According to this interpretation, progress came through technological innovation which raised land productivity (output per acre), and was facilitated by parliamentary enclosure.

The major technological innovations emphasised by this account were two fodder crops, turnips and clover, which gradually became integrated into arable rotations. They increased livestock carrying capacity and therefore supplies of manure – the main fertiliser of arable land. This raised soil fertility and hence yields per acre. The new crops were grown in a rotation in which grain crops alternated with fodder crops, replacing the old rotations in which several grain crops were taken in succession and followed by a bare fallow. The fallow had been necessary to allow nitrogen (an essential plant nutrient) to be restored to the soil from the atmosphere, and also to control perennial weeds by repeated ploughing. Most fallows could be eliminated since weeds could be suppressed

10

by growing turnips provided they were hoed, while clover converted atmospheric nitrogen into nitrates in the soil. A third of the increase in arable productivity in northern Europe between 1750 and 1850 has been attributed to legumes such as clover. Turnips were also instrumental in reclaiming light land that had not previously been cultivated for arable crops. The new crops were often cultivated in a rotation where clover was undersown with barley, and turnips grown as a break between two grain crops. The ultimate expression of these principles was in the Norfolk four-course rotation of wheat, turnips, barley and clover, although the rotation was rarely practised in this pure form. Not all environments were appropriate for it, and even where soils and climate were suitable farmers usually wanted to grow other crops, such as oats to feed their horses.

Other eighteenth-century improvements included the selective breeding of livestock, which changed the size and shape of animals, but more importantly improved the rate at which feed was converted into meat. The widespread introduction of machinery dated from the 1830s and 1840s, although earlier in the century the scythe replaced the sickle as the tool with which wheat was harvested. This change could double labour productivity (output per man) at harvest. Two other nineteenth-century 'agricultural revolutions' have also been proposed: the first dating from the 1830s when the import of feedstuffs and artificial fertilisers from abroad became common, and the second dating from mid-century when the heavy claylands of the country were underdrained using tile drains.

Chambers and Mingay justified these post-1750 changes as 'revolutionary' because they estimated that an additional 6.5 million people were being fed by home production in 1850 compared with 1750. (Population grew by 11 million, but the country switched from being a net exporter of food to a net importer.) Although more land was cultivated, much of this extra food was the result of increased output per acre. Only by increasing land productivity could the country have escaped a 'Malthusian check' in which population growth outstripped the supply of food [Chambers and Mingay (1)].

PERIOD 2: 1650–1750

In a series of articles published in the 1960s A. H. John and E. L. Jones argued independently that rapid technological change in the form of cropping innovations took place in the century after 1650 [Jones (3)]. Although Jones was careful to avoid the phrase, subsequent authors have described these innovations as amounting to an 'agricultural revolution'. In contrast with the following century population growth remained roughly static after 1650, so that the importance of the period lay in a rapid 'transformation in techniques'. These led to increases in grain output per acre, and a rise in total output evidenced by rising grain exports. The processes by which output was increased were virtually the same as for the Chambers and Mingay post-1750 revolution: a rise in the fertility of the soil through turnips and clover and their associated crop rotations. The stimulus for change was seen as a run of sluggish grain prices which squeezed farmers' profits. This caused them to keep more livestock, and more important, to lower unit costs of production by raising yields through the innovation of fodder crops. Landlords supported their tenant farmers and encouraged them to make improvements during this period. If tenant farmers went out of business and no replacements could be found for them, landlords would have been forced to farm the land themselves in order to maintain its condition. Jones also argued for a change in the regional geography of farming, since these new methods were most readily adopted on lightlands – principally the chalk downlands of southern England.

PERIOD 3: 1560–1767, MOST BEFORE 1673

These precise dates come from E. Kerridge whose *Agricultural Revolution* announced, 'This book argues that the agricultural revolution took place in England in the sixteenth and seventeenth centuries and not in the eighteenth and nineteenth' [Kerridge (4)]. Kerridge attempted to establish his claim by dismissing the significance of agricultural change after 1750, and by stressing the importance of technological innovation in

12

the earlier period. He had three lines of attack on the significant features of the traditional post-1750 agricultural revolution. First, he argued that some of them did not occur at all – the mechanisation of farming in the eighteenth century for example. Second, he considered some features to be 'irrelevant' (including parliamentary enclosure, the replacement of bare fallows, the Norfolk four-course, and selective breeding). Third, he maintained that some technological innovations occurred much earlier, such as the introduction of fodder crops, new crop rotations, and field drainage. While some of these points are accepted (farming was not mechanised in the eighteenth century for example), few historians accept his cavalier dismissal of so many features as 'irrelevant'.

After this demolition Kerridge then constructed an argument for an agricultural revolution in this period on the basis of seven criteria which form chapter headings for his book: up and down husbandry, fen drainage, fertilisers, floating the watermeadows, new crops, new systems, and new stock. Most emphasis was placed on up and down husbandry (also called convertible or ley husbandry), in which the distinction between permanent grass and permanent tillage was broken and grass was rotated round the farm, so increasing fertility. Once again the criteria are technological and Kerridge justified his claim for an agricultural revolution by pointing to the fact that domestic agricultural production coped with a doubling of the English population between 1550 and 1750.

NEW RESEARCH

Most research into agrarian history published during the last 20 years or so contributes in some way to the discussion of these three 'agricultural revolutions' but most scholars have avoided direct entanglement with the debate. Taken as a whole, the conclusions of this research are equivocal; no single period emerges as the most likely candidate for the revolutionary label. Space precludes detailed discussion of the individual contributions but some examples may be given.

There is general agreement that Kerridge exaggerates his case for the period 1540–1673. More particularly it has been

13

shown that while convertible husbandry did spread in midland England before the mid-seventeenth century, there was a reversion to permanent pasture after that date. This suggests that part of Kerridge's agricultural revolution may not have been an enduring phenomenon. It has also been shown that population growth ceased about 1650 [Wrigley (6)], and it has been suggested that this amounts to a Malthusian 'preventive check' in that food output was not keeping up with the increase in population.

The most recent verdict on the following period (1640–1750) in *The Agrarian History of England and Wales Volume V* is that a depression in grain prices prompted innovation and enterprise, but that the full harvest of this ingenuity in the form of an agricultural revolution was not to be reaped until after 1750. The view that this period witnessed the most significant changes is supported by recent work by historical demographers. This has shown that from the 1540s onwards there was a positive relationship between the rate of population growth and the rate of growth in food prices: when population grew food prices rose, and when population fell food prices fell. But then, during the 25-year period after 1781, this crucial relationship changed: the rate of population growth remained unprecedentedly high, but the rate of growth in food prices fell. This change indicates that there was some significant increase in agricultural production in this period. Dr Turner presents some corroboratory evidence in the following chapter, in so far as he shows how increases in land productivity could be a consequence of parliamentary enclosure taking place after 1750. On the other hand, this is still a matter of controversy given that recent work by Crafts (see below) contradicts this, and suggests that growth in agricultural output was more rapid in the first half of the eighteenth century than afterwards.

MEASURING AGRICULTURAL CHANGE

These contradictory findings arise in part because of difficulties in measuring the phenomena under discussion. None of the arguments for the three agricultural revolutions outlined above is backed up by comprehensive statistics of innovation, yields, or output. Such estimates may be made in two ways; from the 'top down' and from the 'bottom up'.

The former involve calculating rates of growth in agricultural output at a national level by the application of some basic economic assumptions. Agricultural prices are assumed to be determined by the interaction of the demand and supply of agricultural products. Thus the unknown supply (or output) can then be inferred from the available information on demand (represented by population growth) and on prices. Using such methods Crafts finds that progress was more rapid from 1700 to 1760 than in the latter part of the century. He calculates that agricultural output was growing at 6.2 per cent per decade between 1700 and 1760, but only at 4.5 per cent per decade from 1760 to 1800 [Crafts (2)].

'Bottom up' methods involve the systematic analysis of conventional historical sources (such as probate inventories) at the local or regional level. An example of this approach includes the calculation of crop yields per acre for two counties, Norfolk and Suffolk, together with estimates of the area and output of grain, for the period 1580–1740 [Overton (5)].

Table 1 shows these yield figures, as well as some national estimates for the nineteenth century. The most reliable estimates are those for 1801 and after, and unfortunately the figure for 1750 is little more than a guess. Nevertheless these figures are of considerable interest since all three agricultural revolutions place such strong emphasis on output increases brought about by yield changes. The table suggests that until 1801 increases in yields were steady rather than spectacular; and the most striking feature is the apparent slow-down in the

Table 1   Estimates of wheat yields, 1520–1851 (ten year averages in bushels per acre)

Norfolk & Suffolk		England	
1520	9–11	1750	15–20
1600	11–13	1801	20
1630	12–14	1831	23
1670	14–16	1851	32
1700	14–17		

rate of growth in output per acre between 1750 and 1830. This is not to say that total output was not increasing. On the contrary it was probably growing rapidly as the arable acreage was increased, but average yields did not rise because more and more physically marginal land was brought into cultivation.

Statistics of innovation have also been produced, although again they refer to just two counties. Turnips and clover spread very rapidly amongst the farmers of Norfolk and Suffolk in the century after 1660; by 1720 half the farmers in the two counties were growing root crops, lending considerable support to the argument for an agricultural revolution during that period. Yet appearances can be deceptive. Although turnips were widely grown they were not being cultivated in such a way as to have much impact on grain yields – only some 9 per cent of the cropped acreage of the two counties was under turnips and 3.5 per cent under clover in the 1720s, whereas by the 1850s the percentage for both crops had risen to 20 [Overton (5)]. It is unlikely, therefore, that the crops were *introduced* with the intention of cutting costs through raising grain yields as Jones argues; it is *after* 1750 that fodder crops become important in this way.

PROCESSES OF AGRARIAN CHANGE

This evidence from Norfolk and Suffolk emphasises that the presence of new fodder crops is not in itself sufficient evidence for major technological change; much depends on how they were grown and in what quantities. In fact new rotations involving fodder crops were only one mechanism by which output could have risen. So it is important to distinguish four methods by which the supply of food could have increased:

(i) *The area under cultivation could be extended* so that more grain was grown. This does not necessarily involve any technological change, and it can only be a short-term solution for eventually the supply of land runs out. Although output increases, yields per acre need not rise and could even fall if lower quality land was brought into cultivation.

16

(ii) *Agricultural inputs (such as seed, fertiliser and labour) could be increased* so that existing methods of production were intensified. This need not involve any technological innovation, but would result in a rise in yields. In the long run, however, diminishing returns would mean that an increase in inputs would result in a less than proportionate increase in output.

(iii) *Through regional and local specialisation overall output could increase*; farmers grew the crops that were most suited to the physical environment of their farm. Neither technological change nor an increase in the area cultivated need take place but the overall national output of food could rise.

(iv) *Technological innovations* of the sort already discussed could open the door to unconstrained increases in total output by raising yields per acre.

It should be evident that all four of these mechanisms were in operation, frequently in conjunction, during the centuries under review. For example, the introduction of the Norfolk four-course rotation to raise grain yields is unlikely to have taken place without an extension to the cultivated area. This is because a switch from a three-course rotation (wheat, barley, and fallow) to a four-course (wheat, turnips, barley, and clover) would reduce the *grain area* from two-thirds to one-half of the cropped area and it is unlikely that farmers would have introduced a new rotation to raise grain output if it involved a reduction in the grain area.

THE CONCEPT OF AN AGRICULTURAL REVOLUTION

All three agricultural revolutions under discussion lay strong emphasis on increases in agricultural output, and in two cases on its relationship to a growing population. It is clear, therefore, that this concept of an 'agricultural revolution' needs to take proper account of the mechanisms by which that increase is achieved, since it could be argued that some are more 'revolutionary' than others. Taking a long-term view for example, technological change (method (iv) above) that allows a continued upward spiral in yields is of more signi-

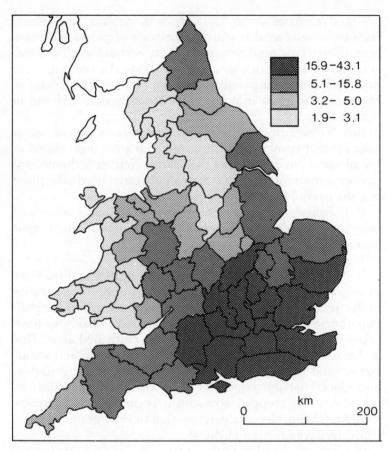

	15.9 – 43.1
	5.1 – 15.8
	3.2 – 5.0
	1.9 – 3.1

Map 1 Ratio of agricultural labourers to farmers who did not employ labour, 1831

ficance than an increase in output brought about by an extension to the cultivated area (method (i)). But given that the phrase 'agricultural revolution' is used simply to refer to a series of events and processes in a particular period which are held to be significant in some sense, there is no reason why the concept should not be applied to other facets of agricultural change. Two of these will be briefly mentioned here.

First, while the productivity of land has been much discussed, comparatively little explicit attention has been paid to the productivity of labour. Yet this is important because an increase in output per man is one of the means by which the post-1750 agricultural revolution contributed to the industrial revolution. If output per worker *in agriculture* rose, a greater proportion of the population could be fed by the agricultural sector, and so be able to work in the *non-agricultural* sector of the economy. No direct figures of labour productivity are available but some indirect estimates can be made. These suggest that output per man in agriculture may have increased by rather more than a third in the century before 1750 and that the pace then accelerated strongly in the following century.

A second theme is the change in the institutional structure of farming. In so far as this is considered at all, it tends to be through the agency of parliamentary enclosure, yet in some ways this may be a red herring. Not only could land be enclosed without act of parliament, but many important processes may well have been independent of parliamentary enclosure. This would apply, for example, to the increase in the size of farms, the concentration of land ownership, the replacement of owner occupiers by tenant farmers, the decline of farm servants, and the establishment of day-labouring as the normal mode of employment.

By the 1830s the three-tiered system of relationships between landlord, tenant farmer, and farm labourer had been established in much of southern England. Map 1 shows the ratio of agricultural labourers to farmers not employing labour (i.e. family farmers). It therefore indicates the very considerable extent to which the agricultural labour force had been proletarianised in many areas, in the sense that people were working on the land for somebody else, rather than for themselves. As a commentator on nineteenth-century Norfolk agriculture put it, 'There is nothing between master and man except work on the one hand and cash on the other'. This change may be regarded as revolutionary. Although it has been discussed in the literature it has received little prominence except in the writings of R. H. Tawney on the sixteenth century, and in the context of the debate on the social consequences of parliamentary enclosure in the eighteenth and nineteenth centuries.

These new findings can form a basis for speculation about agricultural development in the three periods under discussion.

Before 1650 there seem to have been increases both in the area under cultivation and in grain yields, but output per worker did not rise significantly until the 1630s and 1640s. The productivity increase may have been due to the spread of convertible husbandry but it may well have resulted from increased inputs of labour under pressure of population.

During the century after 1650 new crops made a widespread appearance, but probably not in sufficient quantities to have made much impact on yields per acre. Output increases were probably due more to increased regional and local specialisation than to massive technological change.

After 1750 it appears that innovation may have slowed, and the rate of growth in output fallen, as land was converted to pasture with early parliamentary enclosure. After the turn of the nineteenth century more enclosure was for arable farming and, as Dr Turner points out, yields may not have risen because more marginal land was being brought into cultivation. On the other hand, output per agricultural worker was growing rapidly perhaps because of changes in hand tool technology (the scythe) and in the way agricultural labourers were employed.

From 1830 onwards yields per acre increased dramatically, giving a relatively rapid transition to the period of the mid-nineteenth century known as 'high farming'. Innovation continued apace so that for the 18 English counties with data, the proportion of cropland under root crops almost doubled between 1801 and c. 1850, from 11 per cent to just under 20 per cent.

Which was the truly revolutionary era? The answer depends on how the concept of an 'agricultural revolution' is defined. In terms of output per acre the most rapid surge seems to have come after 1831; labour productivity showed a decisive rise after 1801; by 1831 English agriculture was capitalist in structure though sufficient data are not available to enable that particular transition to be charted in detail. The search for an 'agricultural revolution' is as much an exploration of alternative concepts of agrarian change as it is an exploration of the historical record.

REFERENCES AND FURTHER READING

(1) **J. D. Chambers and G. E. Mingay,** *The Agricultural Revolution, 1750–1880* (London, 1966).
(2) **N. F. R. Crafts,** *British Economic Growth during the Industrial Revolution* (Oxford, 1985).
(3) **E. L. Jones,** *Agriculture and the Industrial Revolution* (Oxford, 1974).
(4) **E. Kerridge,** *The Agricultural Revolution* (London, 1967).
(5) **M. Overton,** *Agricultural Revolution in England; the Transformation of the Rural Economy, 1500–1830* (forthcoming Cambridge).
(6) **E. A. Wrigley,** Population growth: England, 1680–1820, *ReFRESH* 1 (1985). Reprinted as Chapter 8 in this volume.

2 Parliamentary Enclosures: Gains and Costs

M. E. TURNER

Recently, historians have reopened many long-standing debates concerning the relationship between land enclosures and economic and social change in eighteenth- and nineteenth-century England. By using a wider range of contemporary documents and employing more rigorous economic and statistical models than before, the perceived backwardness of open-field farming and the productivity gains of enclosures have been re-examined. The social consequences of enclosure are under fresh scrutiny as well, and the ill-effects polemicised in the first decade of the twentieth century, but subsequently refuted, have been reinvestigated and found in many respects to be true.

Enclosure changed agricultural practices which had operated under systems of co-operation in communally administered landholdings, usually in large fields which were devoid of physical territorial boundaries. In their place it created systems in which agricultural holding was on a non-communal, individual basis where man-made boundaries separated one person's land from that of his neighbours. Open-field farming and landownership structure were thereby replaced by individual initiative and individual landholding; specific ownership of land was registered; shared ownership was separated (by identifying common rights of property); and communal obligations, privileges and rights were declared void for all time. Much the same can be said of the counterpart enclosure of commons and wastes [Turner (4) and (5)].

THE EXTENT OF ENCLOSURE

We are concerned here with parliamentary enclosure. This dominated the period from 1750–1830, with remnants reaching into the twentieth century. It was sanctioned by act of parliament, occasioned by private and local petitions and bills for the enclosure of the whole or parts of villages, parishes, townships, and hamlets. The first enclosure act was in 1604 in Radipole in Dorset, but it was not until the mid-eighteenth century that they became so frequent as to warrant measurement (see Figure 1). Private enclosures also took place – local agreements which in previous centuries had often been ratified locally or by the London courts – but after 1750 private enclosure was dwarfed by the statutory instrument. It remains unclear why parliamentary enclosure became dominant; perhaps the subdivision of rights became so complicated

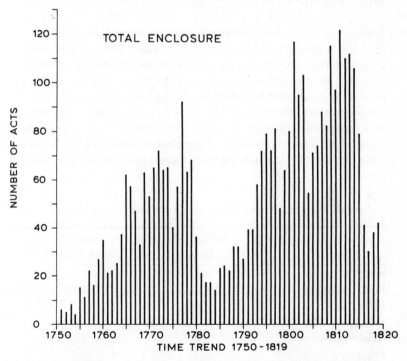

Figure 1 Chronology of parliamentary enclosure in England, 1750–1819

23

with increasing numbers of interested parties that it required a system of referees to separate claims of ownership; or perhaps there was opposition to land reform or squabbling over the redistribution of spoils, making a statutory instrument both necessary and inevitable.

Recourse to parliament has been described as class robbery played according to rules of property which, although fair, were laid down by a parliament of property-owners and lawyers. It has been suggested that the mere fact of applying to parliament is evidence of opposition. These are strong claims and will always be debated. What is without doubt is the physical impact of parliamentary enclosures (see Table 2, Figure 1, and Map 2). There were similar, though less dramatic, land reforms in Wales and Scotland [Turner (5)].

TEMPORAL AND SPATIAL PATTERNS

Until recently it was assumed that parliamentary enclosure had the largest single impact of any other form of enclosure [Wordie (6)]. While the figures of acres enclosed by parliamentary means are not in much dispute, the impact of other periods of enclosure is only partially known. From evidence of parliamentary enclosure itself, and from estimates of private and piecemeal enclosure in the period after 1500, it is possible to build up a partial picture of the disintegration of the former open fields. By estimating the likely acreage of enclosure

Table 2   Statistics of English parliamentary enclosures

	Millions of acres	Area as % of England
Pre-1793	2.6	7.9
1793–1815	2.9	8.9
1816–1829	0.4	1.2
Total pre-1830	5.9	18.0
1830 onwards	0.9	2.9
Total	6.8	20.9

before 1500 and adding this to the post-1500 estimates a grand total of acreage can be calculated. But when this calculation was made it came to only 75 per cent of the land area of England. What of the missing 25 per cent? The author of this calculation [Wordie (6)] ascribes this residual to the only century which is largely unrepresented in the written record, the seventeenth. This produces the following chronology:

Already enclosed in 1500   *c.* 45.0%
enclosed 1500–1599   *c.* 2.0%
enclosed 1600–1699   *c.* 24.0%
enclosed 1700–1799   *c.* 13.0%
enclosed 1800–1914   *c.* 11.4%
commons remaining in 1914   *c.* 4.6%

It is proper to suggest two respects in which these figures deceive the reader, and this can act as a useful reminder of the full impact of parliamentary enclosure. First, if there was that much seventeenth-century enclosure, then unlike other enclosure movements it passed with remarkably little contemporary reporting. More likely, there was more non-parliamentary enclosure throughout the last 500 years than we can assuredly measure. Additionally, to allocate enclosure to broad time periods which are unrelated to the passage of human experience is to misinterpret and understate the impact of parliamentary enclosure in its economic and social setting. 24 per cent of England's land area *may have been enclosed* in the seventeenth century, but 18 per cent *was enclosed* by parliament in two short bursts of activity each of about 20 years duration: in the 1760s and 1770s, and during the French Revolutionary and Napoleonic Wars (see Figure 1).

Secondly, in some counties parliamentary enclosure was negligible (the Welsh borders, and south-east and south-west England); but in others it was massively important (over 50% of Oxfordshire, Northamptonshire and Cambridgeshire was enclosed in less than a century). Enclosure activity was particularly dense in the south and east Midlands and became progressively less important radiating outwards (see Map 2). This reflected the survival by about 1750 of the ancient system of open-field farming [for regional variations see Turner (4)].

This spatial pattern can be related to the chronological

25

pattern. The heavier arable soils of the Midlands were the first to be enclosed in the 1760s and 1770s and much of this arable was converted to grassland farming. The lighter soils still in open fields, and the commons in counties like Cumberland, were enclosed mainly during the French wars, this time in order to extend the arable into marginal lands or to improve the existing arable.

WHY ENCLOSE?

Some motivating forces behind enclosure are revealed in these spatial and temporal patterns. The second quarter of the eighteenth century was a period of depressed prices. There was cheap and plentiful food for a static or slowly growing population, but cheap food at the market meant static or even declining incomes per unit of output for the farmers. In consequence there was a move out of the broadly fixed incomes obtainable from arable farming into the expanding sector of pastoral farming. Demand for meat and dairy products increased, and this gave farmers the opportunity to expand their own incomes by substituting grass for crops. Districts with heavy soils responded first, and a relative profusion of enclosure for conversion to pasture took place. Even in the open fields there were moves to increase the grass acreage. Although prices and farm incomes recovered after 1750 the pattern was already set for heavy-soiled regions to continue moving into grassland farming. Hence the emphasis of parliamentary enclosure in this period in the south and east Midlands.

By the late 1790s the situation had changed dramatically to one of steeply rising prices, led by the increase in corn prices. Enclosure now occurred to take advantage of this. The object was to improve the existing arable in light soiled areas, and extend the arable into marginal areas (marginal economically and also geographically). This pushed the limits of cultivation higher up the mountains and deeper into the wastes. Modern economists identify a statistically testable relationship between price fluctuations and the occurrence of enclosure.

26

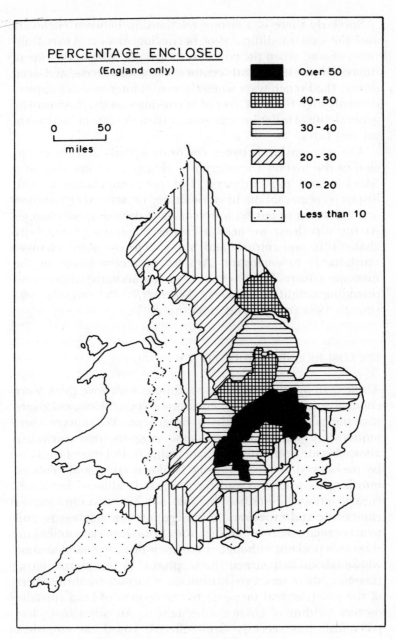

Map 2 Density of parliamentary enclosure in England

Similarly there is a strong relationship between enclosure and the ease or difficulty of borrowing money. Apart from times of war, when the cost of borrowing was high, the rate of interest in the eighteenth century was at low levels, and even during the French wars when the rate of interest was unprecedentedly high the 'real' cost of borrowing was low, because the general rate of inflation was greater than the rate of increase of interest rates.

The relationship between enclosure activity and the extension of the market (demographic change), is somewhat of a 'chicken and egg' mystery. Did prior population growth inspire reorganisation in agriculture, or was reorganisation and extension of output a precursor of demographic change? At the very least we need a clearer picture of productivity changes in agriculture and specific productivity changes attributable to enclosure. Articles in recent issues of the *Economic History Review* explore such questions without yet providing definitive answers. [See *EcHR* 1982 (no. 4), 1983 (no. 2), 1984 (no. 2), and 1985 (no. 3).]

ENCLOSURE AND PRODUCTIVITY

These then are the economic conditions which we think were conducive to investment in enclosure. Nevertheless, enclosure was the action of individuals or groups. What were their motives? A well-established view suggests that enclosure allowed scale economies (i.e. the gains from larger farms) to be introduced by reorganising landownership and tenancy into larger ownership and farm units. It allowed landlords (nearly always described by this old line of argument as capitalistic and rapacious) to renegotiate rents upwards, and to accumulate more of the surpluses from scale economies into their own pockets, although it was their down-trodden tenants whose labour had earned the surpluses. In this simple form, therefore, there was a redistribution of income from the tillers of the soil (the real farmers) to the owners of land (usually owners by dint of chance inheritance). An alternative, less polemical, has recently been offered, based on empirical measurement and economic analysis. It says that the farming community threw off the shackles of the open fields, which were wasteful of land (allowing too frequent fallows), and were restrictive and conservative in operation, with too few crops, too little crop choice, and stylised crop rotations. The newly-liberated countryside produced heavier yields of crops to everyone's advantage. Both of these views have been questioned. There is no evidence that average farm sizes became larger over the course of the eighteenth century *to any considerable degree*, though this does not mean that scale economies and efficiency gains could not develop from enclosures. The landlords could only be as rapacious as their tenants could be efficient. Both landlords and tenants had much to gain from enclosure. Arthur Young was probably right when he observed that both rents and output – landlords' and farmers' incomes – improved in proportion after enclosure.

The debate over the relative efficiencies of open-field and enclosed farming, however, is unresolved. There is evidence both of open-field adaptation to meet changing economic circumstances, and also of backwardness. For Oxfordshire M. Havinden [reprinted in Jones (2)] substantiated the former view in a classic defence of the open fields. Adaptation was so accomplished here that enclosure was held in abeyance until well into the nineteenth century. But this was not the case everywhere. In neighbouring Buckinghamshire unchanging crop and rotation patterns persisted, and farmers' attempts to extend grassland cultivation were frustrated by unbending open-field regulations. Enclosure came decades earlier in north Buckinghamshire than in Oxfordshire. Contemporary evidence shows that open-field farming was a restraint on productivity. There were losses in the open fields due to trespass, the employment of wasteful fallows, and the inefficiency of having scattered holdings. Scattering was 'the evil of bad cultivation', and common-field husbandry 'allowed not of turnipping, nor of any other late and valuable improvements in agriculture' [Turner (4)]. Table 3 compares the different cropping profiles and estimates of productivity per acre (*c.* 1801) for open and enclosed parishes in Northamptonshire, a county which was not untypical in this respect.

We can see from Section A of this table that the enclosed

29

Table 3 Crop distributions, productivity, and grain output in Northamptonshire, circa 1801

	(A) Crop Distribution acres per parish							(B) Productivity bushels per acre			(C) Output bushels per parish			
	wheat	barley	oats	total grain	pulses	roots	total crops	wheat	barley	oats	wheat	barley	oats	total grain
45 parishes in open fields	190.3	164.8	48.9	404.0	178.3	24.8	615.4	17.9	24.0	22.7	3406.4	3955.2	1110.0	8471.6
102 enclosed parishes	141.7	134.5	105.3	381.5	60.4	56.2	509.8	19.5	27.6	27.0	2763.2	3712.2	2843.1	9318.5

Sources: Adapted from the 1801 crop returns in the Public Record Office (HO/67) and a harvest enquiry of 1795 in the Public Record Office (HO/42/36 and 37, 5th and 27th November 1795).

farms had a more even distribution of grain crops; a markedly lower acreage under pulses (such as peas and beans); and a bigger area of root crops. Section B shows the higher grain output per acre obtained by the enclosed farms. Finally, Section C shows that this increase in productivity was more than sufficient to compensate for the lower acreage under grain so that more grain was produced than in the open fields. This allowed the land that was saved to be put to other uses, like grass.

But farming is the business of farmers, and one contemporary reminds us that they were protected from their own bad practice inclinations by those very same communal obligations of open-field agriculture which enclosure sought to remove. Enclosure could certainly make a good farmer better, but it could make these bad ones worse.

SOCIAL CONSEQUENCES

The Hammonds exposed the damaging social consequences of enclosure, because it destroyed the social fabric of village life, and eventually was fatal to three classes; the small farmer, the cottager, and the squatter [Hammonds (1)]. It was argued, in contradiction, that enclosures created more not fewer employment opportunities with the initial construction and subsequent upkeep of hedges and ditches. Furthermore, at an estimated £2 to £3 per acre, enclosure costs were said to be small in relation to the improved value of the land, while the owner could resort to mortgage facilities if necessary. Thus the small farmer, or more especially the independent owner-occupier, was not dealt a savage blow. The architect of this anti-Hammonds line, J. D. Chambers [reprinted in Jones (2)], claimed that the numbers of small owner-farmers actually rose not fell after enclosure. Accordingly, the mechanism which turned a farming rural proletariat into an industrial urban one was not enclosure, but an expanding population. A demographic revolution created more manpower than there were employment opportunities in a relatively fixed-resource countryside. The exodus to the towns, therefore, arose from the push of demography and the pull of urban work, not from the push of enclosure. This view became a virtual orthodoxy. Recently, however, methods of investigation and analysis have swung opinion back towards the Hammonds' view, though without the political and polemical bias they employed.

There were some unequivocally damaging effects of enclosure. By enclosing commonable lands and removing them from general village use – including local rights to depasture animals on the stubble of the arable fields after harvest, and on the fallow field – the landless, who were always the majority in number, were deprived of general access to open places for fuel gathering, tethering and grazing animals, and recreation. After enclosure, such places were either non-existent or greatly reduced in size and numbers. Even those who successfully claimed and were granted land in lieu of common rights found that the land they received was little more than a large (sometimes small!) garden, but a garden which attracted a proportion of enclosure and fencing costs. In reality, enclosure costs, when the unavoidable costs of fencing are included, could be as high as £12 per acre. Many common rights claimants sold up their newly-acquired land at or shortly after enclosure, and lost all semblance of independence, becoming totally wage-dependent. This heightened class consciousness and accelerated social differentiation within the village [Snell, (3)].

Although small owner-occupiers increased in number at enclosure, as Chambers claimed, this is now known to be a distortion of the real events. Before enclosure common rights were vested in non-real property, but at enclosure they were translated into real property (land) thus initially swelling the numbers of 'land' owners. Many of them subsequently sold these newly acquired but excessively small plots. More substantial landowners also found that their ancestral lands had been greatly reduced in size (especially by redeeming or commuting tithes by a once-and-for-all payment of land). Although shedding the tithe was welcomed, their land was often rendered too small for complete independence, and they were also burdened with enclosure and fencing costs. A turnover of property occurred which was closely related to the incidence of enclosure. The Land Tax (which is a record of ownership and occupancy), reveals that in Buckinghamshire, for example, within two or three years of enclosure, 30 to 50 per cent of pre-enclosure landowners sold their land, in comparison with the normal activities of the land market which suggest a turnover rate of less than 20 per cent every decade. In Northamptonshire this turnover was most pronounced among the smallest landowners. The 'head count' only grew through the recognition during enclosure of what was a common right. A failure by Chambers fully to appreciate this point distorted his and others' appraisal of enclosure.

There is also a growing appreciation that there was a mounting record of opposition to enclosure. The Hammonds' famous dictum that 'the suffrages were not counted but weighed', meaning that it was landownership strength measured in property rather than in gross numbers which influenced parliament, has become the reasonable answer to those who claimed that parliamentary enclosure was a process which recognised the rights even of humble men. Finally, it is unlikely that enclosure increased long-term employment outside the immediate task of building fences and ditches. Up to 1780 there was a move to convert arable to pasture, involving a transition from a more to a less labour-intensive system. Much enclosure before 1780, therefore, was probably labour shedding.

ECONOMIC GAINS BUT SOCIAL COSTS

Enclosure certainly shook the countryside up, but demographic change, especially after 1780, is still much the most likely candidate for the emergence of a rural proletariat which tramped to the towns. Enclosure lubricated the process, but was not its sole nor necessarily main cause. The missing link is the role agriculture played in the process of demographic change. Agriculture became more efficient in the late seventeenth and eighteenth centuries, and enclosure was one contributory improvement. But did this efficiency promote improvements in living standards, or did agriculture respond to such changes which were already in train? This is certainly the next important question to raise, and it may be answered by investigating at local levels the changes which took place in land management. In this way future research may disentangle the productivity changes that actually occurred, from the latent potential for further improvements that was frustrated by the persistence of an open-field system at a time of population increase.

REFERENCES AND FURTHER READING

(1) **J. L. and B. Hammond,** *The Village Labourer* (London, 1911 and reprinted 1980).
(2) **E. L. Jones,** *Agriculture and Economic Growth in England 1650–1815* (London, 1967), essays by J. D. Chambers and M. Havinden.
(3) **K. D. M. Snell,** *Annals of the Labouring Poor: Social Change and Agrarian England 1660–1900* (Cambridge, 1985), chapter 4.
(4) **M. E. Turner,** *English Parliamentary Enclosure: Its Historical Geography and Economic History* (Folkestone, 1980).
(5) **M. E. Turner,** *Enclosures in Britain 1750–1830* (London, 1984).
(6) **J. R. Wordie,** 'The Chronology of English Enclosure, 1500–1914', *Economic History Review*, 2nd series, vol. XXXVI, no. 4 (1983).
(7) **J. M. Neeson,** 'The Opponents of Enclosure in Eighteenth-Century Northamptonshire', *Past and Present*, 105 (1984).
(8) **M. E. Turner,** 'English Open Fields and Enclosures: Retardation or Productivity Improvements', *Journal of Economic History*, XLVI (1986).
(9) **J. Chapman,** 'The Extent and Nature of Parliamentary Enclosure', *Agricultural History Review*, 35 (1987).

3 The Highland Clearances

T. M. DEVINE

The Highland Clearances were the process by which between
c. 1760 and c. 1860 the inhabitants of entire districts in the
Scottish Highlands and Islands were displaced and evicted
from their lands. It is one of the classic themes of Scottish
history but also of much more general historiographical significance. The subject offers an unrivalled opportunity for an
examination of the social consequences of agrarian modernisation. The Clearances bring into particularly sharp focus the
titanic conflict between the forces of peasant traditionalism
and agrarian rationalism. All the great themes are there: the
powers of the landed classes; the constraints of economic and
demographic pressure; dispossession; peasant resistance; cultural alienation; migration and emigration.

BEFORE THE CLEARANCES

Any assessment of the social impact of the Clearances vitally
depends on some reckoning of conditions in the Highlands
before the evictions began. Nineteenth-century critics argued
that the majority of the population lived a secure and relatively
comfortable existence which was later irreparably damaged
by dispossession. Modern research has painted a quite different picture. Before 1750 the evidence suggests that the northern region, even by the standards of the rest of Scotland, was
very poor; that its economy was precariously balanced between meagre sufficiency and intermittent shortage; that
destitution was widespread and the people endured a constant
struggle in a land of uncertain climate, limited arable resources and poor natural endowment. The Clearances did not

35

in themselves cause Highland poverty; that was an inevitable fact of life, long before the later eighteenth century [Richards (1), Gray (2)].

VARIETIES OF CLEARANCE

The great evictions are commonly viewed in particularly stark and simple terms. It is still widely held that the Clearances refer to the process of wholesale expulsion of entire communities through the use of especially brutal methods, in order to clear land for the formation of large sheep ranches. While such a description does have validity when applied to many evictions at certain periods, it is essentially an over-simplification of a much more complex social development. Easy generalisation is impossible because each 'clearance' had individual characteristics dictated by landlord attitudes, and the varied influence of demographic and economic pressures.

Some removals occurred through a discreet and gradual thinning of the ranks of the small tenantry, in the manner reminiscent of many other parts of Britain in the age of agricultural improvement that has been discussed in the preceding chapters. There were striking differences in the scale, speed and modes of dispossession. Eviction was only one of a series of sanctions employed: others included confiscation of the cattle stock of those in arrears; controls over subdivision of land; refusal of famine relief. Some proprietors went to considerable lengths to accommodate displaced populations; others evicted without compunction or concern for the social costs of their actions. In the later eighteenth century it was common to plan for a redistribution of the population; after *c.* 1820 the strategy more often became one of an undisguised determination to expel. These different approaches were responses to the varied economic and social incentives and pressures of the period 1760–1860. They ensured that the phrase 'the Highland Clearances' is 'an omnibus term to include any kind of displacement by Highland landlords; it does not discriminate between small and large evictions, voluntary and forced removals, or between outright expulsion of tenants and re-settlement' [Richards (1)].

36

The fact that the Clearances were far from homogeneous either in origin or effect renders meaningful analysis very difficult. Some attempt, however, can be made to categorise them roughly in a more coherent manner in order to move towards a definition of particular phases and types of eviction. In very broad terms, therefore, five classes of clearance may be identified.

(i) The southern and eastern Highlands

Between c. 1780 and c. 1830, along the arable fringes of the Highlands in eastern Inverness, southern Argyllshire, Easter Ross and parts of Sutherland, the existing structure was dissolved and replaced by a pattern of larger farms, held by one man, employing wage labourers. Alongside the new order emerged a 'croft' or smallholding system which became a source of seasonal labour for the large units and also an efficient means of bringing marginal land into steady cultivation. Eviction of small tenants and sub-tenants was a central part of the process but these 'clearances' had less harmful results than elsewhere because the new agriculture was founded on a combination of mixed husbandry and pastoral specialisation. Thus the dispossessed were often absorbed within the labour-intensive regime of arable cropping or in the developing crofting structure [Gray (2)].

(ii) Cattle farming

For the most part the rearing of black cattle for sale in southern markets was accommodated within the traditional economic and social structure of the Highlands. This was in contrast to commercial sheep-farming which almost from its inception fell under the control of capitalist farmers from the Lowland and Border counties. Nevertheless, in some districts, extensive cattle ranches were established in response to external market pressures and many small tenants in consequence turned out of their holdings. This pattern was widely noted in a significant number of parishes in Dunbartonshire, Argyll and Perth as early as the 1750s [Richards (1)].

Map 3   Scotland: showing place names in the text

(iii) The creation of the Croft System

Throughout the western mainland north of the Ardnamur-chan peninsula and the inner and outer Hebrides, the existing system of joint tenancies and communal agriculture was terminated beween *c.* 1760 and *c.* 1840. This region afforded only limited possibilities for arable or mixed farming and therefore lacked the potential for the moderate land consolidation and the formation of medium-sized farms characteristic of the southern and eastern Highlands and the Scottish Lowlands. Here the landlord strategy was devoted to the formation of individual smallholdings or 'crofts' which were allocated in 'townships' or crofting settlements [Hunter (3)]. It is important to stress that this change did not destroy the peasant class though it did dramatically affect status, size of holding and local distribution of population. Essentially it perpetuated the connection with land and, within the croft system, subdivision of units among kinfolk became commonplace. Yet, while the formation of the new structure did not possess the drama associated with the more notorious evictions for sheep-farming, it did result in substantial disruption, displacement and relocation of population. Over less than two generations it transformed the entire social map and pattern of settlement of the western Highlands and Islands. One expression of the social resentment which the process produced was the great wave of transatlantic emigrations which were triggered by it after *c.* 1760 and which predated the arrival of the large sheep farms by several decades [Bumstead (4)].

(iv) Sheep-farming

Commercial sheep-farming penetrated the southern and eastern counties of the region in the last quarter of the eighteenth century. After 1800 the pace of development quickened significantly. Inverness had a sheep stock of 50,000 at that date; by 1880 it had reached 700,000. The speed of expansion in Sutherland was even more rapid. That county had only about 15,000 sheep in 1811 but 130,000 nine years later. Almost inevitably pastoral husbandry practised on this huge scale would result in far-reaching population displacement. Commercial pastoralism was conducted most efficiently in large units: the conventional wisdom had it that the most economical ratio was a single shepherd to 600 sheep. Again, the big farmers who controlled the business required the low-lying areas of arable on which the peasant communities clustered. At the very core of their operations was the vital need for suitable land for wintering in the harsh climate of the northern mountains. On this depended both the quality and the quantity of stock which they could maintain. The consequence was a sweeping increase in clearance: 'Where dispossessed families had been numbered in tens before, now there were hundreds. Kintail, Glenelg, Glendessary, and Loch Arkaig ... names of bitter memory plot the movements of the sheep farming frontier' [Gray (2)].

Although these removals often resulted in emigration they did not necessarily cause wholesale depopulation, until at least the second decade of the nineteenth century. Frequently the dispossessed were relocated on coastal or marginal areas while the interior glens were laid down for sheep. The best known example of this pattern was the great clearances in Sutherland where between c. 1810 and c. 1825 an estimated 8,000 to 9,000 people were moved to the coastal fringe and settled in fishing and quasi-industrial communities. This was probably the most remarkable programme of social engineering ever undertaken in nineteenth-century Britain. In the short run, at least, it limited out-migration but, in the longer term, population levels on the estate began to fall rapidly.

(v) Emigration and clearance

Between c. 1840 and c. 1860 a new series of evictions began in the western Highlands and Islands. They differed from most previous clearances since they were intended to achieve depopulation. Attempts at resettlement were abandoned and increasingly those displaced were encouraged to emigrate. 'Compulsory emigration', to use the contemporary phrase, became widespread. Landlords offered the bleak choice to their small tenantry of eviction or dispossession together with assisted passage to North America or Australia. During the potato famines of the period 1846–56 an estimated 16,000

40

received assistance to emigrate in this way from either proprietors or charitable societies.

PRECONDITIONS FOR CLEARANCE

A useful approach here might be to consider initially those
general, conditioning factors which made widespread population displacement possible. This can then be followed by an
analysis of those influences which triggered the specific types
of clearance outlined earlier in the essay.

The Jacobite defeat in 1746 and the imposition of effective
rule by the state officially brought to an end the old clan-based
martial society of the Highlands. Land could now more easily
be regarded as a unit of resource than the basis of military
power. This created the essential precondition for rationalisa-
tion of traditional agriculture. Landlords more than ever
before came to value their estates principally as economic
assets. It is important, however, not to exaggerate the significance of the aftermath of the '45 rebellion. Rather than a
great watershed it can more reasonably be seen in the light of
recent research as the final phase in the steady encroachment
of state power in the Highlands, a process which can be traced
back at least to the reign of James VI and I in the early
seventeenth century. It is now clear also that southern civilisa-
tion and economic pressure were already influencing the
mentalité of Highland proprietors, the markets for Highland
products, such as cattle, fish and timber, and even tenurial
structures in some districts long before 1745 [Hunter (3)].
Finally, there was no automatic link between pacification and
clearance. Major structural change did not begin in the
Highlands for about two decades or more after Culloden,
indicative of the fact that the massive expansion in the
markets for northern commodities in the last quarter of the
eighteenth century was much more decisive in initiating
innovation than political change.

Landlord authority was a vital precondition of the Clearances. If, as is often asserted, Scottish landowners were among
the most powerful in Europe, the Highland élite was the most
absolute of all. They had enormous capacity to displace

41

population and radically alter settlement structure. The peasantry possessed land but did not own it; there were therefore few of the obstacles which restrained seigneurial power in many European societies. The vast majority of the small tenantry had no leases and held land on an annual basis. Below this rent-paying group, and forming as much as one third to one half of the population of some estates in the nineteenth century, was an undermass of semi-landless sub-tenants who paid no rent directly to the proprietor. Most inhabitants on a typical Highland property were therefore liable to eviction at the landlord's will. There were none of the complicated legal procedures associated with the enclosure of lands in England. Landowners merely had to obtain a Summons or Writ of Removal from the local Sheriff Court.

These tenurial weaknesses reflected the absence of bargaining power on the part of the small tenantry. With the expansion of capital-intensive commercial pastoralism, they rapidly ceased to have much economic value. The balance of power swung even more emphatically towards the proprietor in the subsistence crises of 1816–17, 1837–38 and, most importantly, the great potato famine of 1846–56. Many came to depend at these times on the largesse of landlords for life itself. With few legal, tenurial or economic restraints on the autocracy of the social élite, the relationship between proprietor and the small tenantry could easily become an exploitative one. Only sustained and stubborn resistance in the fashion of the Irish peasantry might have inhibited the full implementation of landlord strategies but, although modern research shows that the Clearances were far from peaceful, effective and enduring protest before 1860 was relatively rare [Richards (1)]. The problem was, however, that even in times of severe destitution the crofters and cottars only grudgingly surrendered their land; contemporary observers also pointed out that the poorest class in the Highlands was also the least mobile. As the great French historian, Pierre Goubert, has said: 'No peasant willingly gives up land, be it only half a furrow'. Out of the inevitable conflict between landlord omnipotence and these unyielding peasant values came the agony of the Clearances.

Illustration 1 A dwelling in Skye, 1853 (Illustrated London News, 15 January 1853)

43

Within this general context it is possible to identify three specific influences which contributed directly to population displacement at different times between 1760 and 1860.

(i) The landlord role

Pressure on the landlord class to exploit their estates more effectively intensified in the later eighteenth century due to the impact of 'improving' ideology, the growing hostility to communal practices and structures, the new faith in individualism and the increasing costs of maintaining social position in an age of rising inflation and competitive display. The Highland aristocracy had fewer choices and alternatives than their peers elsewhere in Britain due to the poverty of the resource base in the north, the virtual absence of coal reserves, the weakness of the urban sector and the very great suitability of the area for large-scale commercial pastoralism.

(ii) The expansion of markets

Growing landlord needs for more income coincided with a huge expansion in demand from the urban and industrialising areas of Britain for all Highland produce. The markets for cattle, sheep, whisky, fish, timber, slate and kelp were all buoyant. Increases in production of some of these commodities, notably cattle, could often be accommodated within the existing social and settlement structure. But sheep and kelp were less easily absorbed. Kelp manufacture was the highly labour-intensive production of alkali from seaweed which was used in the soap and glass industries. By 1815 it was reckoned to employ between 25,000 to 30,000 in the western Highlands and Islands. Landlords broke up the existing joint tenancies to create subsistence plots for both the kelp labour force and for fishermen [Hunter (3)]. Large-scale sheep-farming caused even greater displacement. The local population was mainly excluded; the new breeds were Cheviots and Lintons from the south and sheep-ranching quickly became a business of great efficiency absorbing large amounts of capital in which traditional society was very deficient. As the sheep frontier expanded, communities were uprooted and resettled in less favoured areas.

(iii) Economic and demographic strain

From the 1820s serious economic recession undermined many of the peasant bi-employments of the period before 1815. Fishing stagnated, cattle prices fell and above all kelp manufacture collapsed with the rise of the modern chemical industry and the removal of excise duty on salt. At the same time the population of the western Highlands and Islands continued to increase at a rate per annum which accelerated from 0.72 (1801–10) to 1.46 (1811–20) before falling to 0.51 (1821–30). The signs of escalating demographic strain were clearly revealed in the subsistence crises of 1816–17, 1837–38 and 1846–56. This was the background to a new wave of clearances through which landlords sought to remove the 'redundant' population because they feared the huge burden of relief costs in maintaining the people and increasingly saw no viable economic alternative to large-scale sheep husbandry. In a sense, this recognition simply reflected the imperatives of developing regional specialisation within the British economy and the tendency of many areas to move towards exploitation of comparative advantage.

THE SOCIAL RESPONSE

The Highland Clearances were associated with protest, trauma and bitterness when they occurred and bequeathed to posterity a popular tradition of lost rights and wrongful dispossession. Much recent work has focused on the reasons why agrarian reorganisation in the Highlands caused a deeper sense of alienation than anywhere else in Britain.

One likely explanation is that many of the evictions in the Highlands had more serious social costs than consolidation of land in other areas. The drive towards the expansion of commercial pastoralism created particularly large farms which were both capital- and land-intensive but had little need for many hands. The new agrarian sector excluded the local population while at the same time it monopolised much of the scarce arable lands and absorbed the pastures of the old peasant cattle economy. While the mixed husbandry of the southern and eastern Highlands, and in the Scottish Lowlands, released employment opportunities, sheep-farming, in particular, almost invariably led to the contraction of peasant resources and income.

The problem of absorbing the cleared populations was rendered even more acute by the fact that no permanent alternative to agriculture emerged in the region. Despite the efforts of several proprietors, southern business interests and even government, the infant industrial growths of the later eighteenth century withered in the recession after the Napoleonic Wars under the impact of intense competition from Lowland manufacturing centres. No dynamic urban or industrial sector developed, as in central Scotland, to absorb the dispossessed. Their sufferings were rendered even more traumatic by the fact that evictions tended increasingly to concentrate in years of subsistence crisis. At these times, hunger, disease and loss of land combined to cause terrible social destitution throughout the western mainland and islands [Hunter (3)].

There was also something distinctive about the nature of many clearances in the Highlands. They occurred within a predominantly peasant society in which, until the 1840s and beyond, land remained the primary source of food, fuel, drink, clothing and shelter. There was a widespread belief in the 'right to land', a claim which had no legal foundation but which may have rested on the ancient clan tradition of dispensing land in return for service. Ironically the old martial ethos survived in a new form long after the Jacobite defeat at Culloden, because of the landlord custom of raising regiments from the men of their estates for the British army, through the simple expedient of promising land in return for service. Not surprisingly after 1800, the assumption persisted on several properties that the right to the secure possession of land had been acquired in return for service not in the distant past but in the very recent present. Partly because of this the land issue stirred deeper passions in Gaeldom than anywhere else in Britain.

Yet, it was precisely in this society that eviction took place very rapidly on an especially enormous scale. This was partly because the new sheep and cattle ranches demanded huge areas of land and partly because removal could be accomplished relatively easily with minimal legal fuss. But it was also related to the phasing of agrarian change, especially along the west coast and the islands. Two coherent processes can be identified. The first, roughly covering the period *c*. 1760 to 1820, involved the concentration of a larger population than before along the coasts. The second, from about the 1820s to the 1850s, moved to the opposite extreme, to the consolidation of land and the dispersal of many communities. Draconian methods were widely employed in this phase to expel dense communities of smallholders. It was from this period and these districts that much of the sense of bitterness associated with the Clearances derives. These evictions also stirred emotions outside the Highlands because they were still taking place as late as the 1850s and were widely publicised. Thus this evoked the sympathies of an age with a more sensitive social conscience, a growing hostility to the excesses of landlord authority and a developing 'romantic' interest in Highland society. It was partly this growth in public sympathy which enabled Gladstone's government in 1886 to pass the Crofters' Holding Act, which considerably checked the powers of landlordism and provided for the crofting population the right to secure possession of land for which they had so long craved.

CONCLUSIONS

This topic is still at a relatively immature stage of historical investigation. There is a major need for both detailed empirical research and conceptual development in the methodology of analysis. A series of professional local studies of the type common in France would be most useful. No economic history of sheep-farming exists. Detailed studies of individual estates and of key phases in the processes of eviction would be very welcome. A systematic evaluation of the linkages between eviction, migration and emigration is a major requirement. However, it is already reasonably clear that the Clearances varied significantly over time and place, had complex origins and were not simply the result of the imposition of overweening landlord authority on a dependent peasantry. It is also firmly established that population displacement in the Highlands was mainly a consequence rather than a cause of the poverty and social distress of the region. At worst, the Clearances aggravated conditions of destitution which existed before they took place and which were then exacerbated by the combined influence of limited natural endowment, regional specialisation, rising population and weak economic diversification.

REFERENCES AND FURTHER READING

(1) **E. Richards,** *A History of the Highland Clearances: Agrarian Transformation and the Evictions, 1746–1886* (London, 1982).
(2) **M. Gray,** *The Highland Economy, 1750–1850* (Edinburgh, 1957).
(3) **J. Hunter,** *The Making of the Crofting Community* (Edinburgh, 1976).
(4) **J. M. Bumstead,** *The Peoples Clearance: Highland Emigration to British North America 1770–1815* (Edinburgh, 1982).
(5) **E. Richards,** *The Leviathan of Wealth* (London, 1973).
(6) **P. Gaskell,** *Morvern Transformed* (Cambridge, 1968).
(7) **A. J. Youngson,** *After the Forty Five* (Edinburgh, 1973).
(8) **T. M. Devine,** *The Great Highland Famine: Hunger, Emigration and the Scottish Highlands in the Nineteenth Century* (Edinburgh, 1988).
(9) **A. I. Macinnes,** 'Scottish Gaeldom: the First Phase of Clearance', in T. M. Devine and R. Mitchison (eds), *People and Society in Scotland, 1760–1830* (Edinburgh, 1988).

II Economy

4 Domesday Book after 900 Years

S. HARVEY

The nine-hundredth centenary of the compilation of Domesday Book has made it the focus of much attention. It has always been agreed that Domesday Book was an exceptionally rich source of historical information, but there has been long-standing controversy about the purpose for which it was compiled, the extent to which it revealed continuities or change between Anglo-Saxon and Norman England, and the accuracy of its detailed estimates of wealth and taxpaying capacity. In this chapter we evaluate the answers which modern research has brought to these and related questions.

Domesday Book was unique in Western Europe and it set a standard: henceforward only the most all-embracing surveys were called Domesday. What is known as Domesday Book is in fact a composite work in two volumes. Volume one, known as Great or Exchequer Domesday, is an abbreviated version of the returns from 32 counties; while volume two, or Little Domesday, covers the counties of Essex, Norfolk and Suffolk, and gives all the details of the original findings. The Inquiry also had many local detailed versions and extracts. Much of the data are numerical, and the whole is written in a highly abbreviated and shorthand Latin. It thus bulks large in our information on early Norman England, and on the late Anglo-Saxon England taken over by the Normans. For the economic and social historian there are valuable data on arable exploitation and on annual incomes from landholding, and also an enumeration of rural population in different classes from which subsequent population trends in England can be measured. For historians of government, Domesday Book represents in its framework the evidence for many of the procedures of administration.

Historians have argued for a long time on why and how Domesday Book came to be written. It has no title page, no author, no editor, no preface. And it probably did not get its name until a few decades had passed. The mystery of the precise intentions behind this immense administrative effort has been investigated along with its methods. Arguments as to *why* it was made have been based on *how* it was made. This can be confusing as these are potentially two different subjects. Just as important, before the contents of Domesday can be put to use, we need to know their origin and bias. The question mark which hangs over the rule of Norman England in general hangs over Domesday Book in particular. What role did surviving Anglo-Saxon institutions play in its make-up? What is the product of new forces and new rulers?

Controversy has focused on two related issues: the nature of the institutions – whether Saxon or Norman – involved in the compilation of the information for Domesday Book; and its purpose. Was it designed as a tax book, with the data assembled on the basis of 'hundreds', a geographical area; or for the levy of feudal obligations, with the data assembled on the basis of 'tenants-in-chief', a group of landholders at the summit of the feudal hierarchy? (For a brief explanation of these terms, and of others shown in quotation marks, see the box.)

About the turn of the century much careful research was carried out on Domesday Book. The Victorian scholars – J. H. Round and F. W. Maitland – both concluded Domesday was nothing other than a tax or 'geld' book. They did so chiefly on the evidence from a 'satellite source', the Inquest of the County of Cambridge, which is laid out by hundreds. Information was provided by juries – representatives on oath – from the hundreds (an Anglo-Saxon institution) probably in the shire court (also Anglo-Saxon) to gather information for a tax reassessment. This country-wide Anglo-Saxon taxation was unique in Western Europe, and was perhaps the main reason why England was so attractive to the invasion of would-be kings. The assembly of information was overseen by groups of royal commissioners: trusted leading Normans, both

Demesne: lands not let out to tenants.

Geld: literally 'money' but used for all sorts of taxes. 'The geld' denotes the national system of taxation.

Hundred: the administrative unit within the shire in the south and west of England.

Satellites: texts associated with the Domesday Inquiry, but with their exact relationship undetermined.

Tenants-in-chief: the leading barons who held land from the king.

Thegns: Anglo-Saxon gentry.

Vills: a feudal township consisting of a number of houses or buildings with their adjacent lands.

Wapentake: the local administrative unit in the Danelaw, equivalent to the hundred.

ecclesiastics and laymen. Thus, according to this view, the Inquiry was the product of Anglo-Saxon institutions taken over by the new Norman ruling group to revitalise a long-established tax system.

The character of Domesday that V. H. Galbraith propounded in 1940 was completely different. He argued that it was an inquiry of feudal 'tenants-in-chief' for a feudal purpose, *not* for the collection of geld. His chief source was another 'satellite', the Exeter Domesday, with its original livestock detail laid out under tenants-in-chief, and crossing the boundaries not only of hundreds, but even of counties. Galbraith argued that Domesday Book represented the revolution in tenure that had taken place in England, because it consisted of returns by 'tenants-in-chief', who were mostly new and mostly Norman. In his view its purpose was to obtain a valuation of their lands upon which feudal obligations would be levied. These included the lord's right to take the lands of a minor or heiress into his own hands during the minority, or before marriage, for wardship: in practice this meant he would take the bulk of the income from the land himself. According to this view Domesday Book's inspiration was thus new and Norman and feudal.

The disadvantage of both these theories is that they cannot easily be reconciled with the order of Domesday Book itself. Domesday Book is actually a sandwich of the two approaches. It is laid out first by counties, then within counties by tenants-in-chief, then within the lands of the tenants-in-chief, by hundreds. The two units are not self-contained: many tenants-in-chief held lands in several counties, and in different hundreds in a single county: some 'vills' were divided amongst several holders. How was this information assembled? Both the theories outlined above would require a major reordering of material and a complete rewriting to produce the order of Domesday Book. But time was short. The consensus reached by modern historians is that both Domesday volumes were produced in William's reign, not later: the inquiry was completed in 1086, and the king saw the returns before he left England for the last time in August. The refined version of Great Domesday was produced in the following twelve months, and when William died in September 1087, work on it stopped with the cities of London and Winchester not yet copied up. How can this be resolved?

SOLUTION AND RESOLUTION

I would argue that the departure point of the inquiry was shire lists already in existence for tax purposes. These formed the skeletal framework for Domesday since such lists were already arranged both in order of landholder and in order of hundred, sometimes the landholder was primary and sometimes the hundred. Most survive in copies in the archives of landholders and can be dated *before* Domesday Book: either they contain earlier assessment figures or they show an earlier situation in landholdings. Within Domesday itself survive lists for Yorkshire, previously thought of as summaries of Domesday. One section dealing with royal lands is arranged under landholders of the 1060s (including Earl Tostig who died in 1065) and another section is arranged by 'wapentakes' with the holders of land annotated in. Such fiscal lists emphasise the force of the Anglo-Saxon foundations of Domesday Book. They also show that the great landholders knew their fiscal responsibility before, as well as after, the Conquest. That is not to ignore the large contribution of the landholders. Much of the detailed information was probably supplied directly by the larger landholders, but provided according to the shire lists supplied. Probably the hundred was primary in the east of the country and the landholder in the west. Either way the information was quickly converted to the other order.

We now turn to the second issue: the function of Domesday Book. On this, Galbraith's view – that it was a feudal valuation – has won consensus. The annual values of estates undoubtedly interested the commissioners most; the values were the sole item given for the two dates with the utmost consistency, and in 18 counties they are often given for a third, interim date as well. The feudal valuation is the one entirely novel purpose of Domesday Book, fully intentional, and fully carried out. The whole character of William II's reign (and much of Henry I's Coronation Charter), is a commentary on this use of Domesday. With the knowledge of the values of his tenants-in-chief before him William II could be ruthlessly demanding because he could be precise. Indeed, knowing the values of ecclesiastical lands, he could hardly bear to let them out of his hands at all: he deliberately kept at least eight bishoprics and thirteen abbeys vacant so that he could receive their revenues.

The vast Domesday data also indicate a second function. An almost complete turn-over in landholding had taken place forcefully in the previous twenty years; military men had even moved into the one stable element, the lands of the churches. Undoubtedly a second and vital function of the Inquiry was to check the authority of these tenurial changes. Disputes were not necessarily resolved, but they were recorded for settlement subsequently, and in some counties long lists of disputes are recorded in Domesday Book. Particular inquiries to deal with disputed lands had already been held in William's reign, consisting of sessions of royal commissioners with representatives of shires and hundreds present. To check landholding was a central function of the Inquiry without which valuation or fiscal reassessment would be useless.

Thirdly, Domesday Book *was* intended to be a geld book. But not for the collection of geld, it had been collected long before the Domesday Inquiry; and not for an arbitrary and *ad hoc* reassessment. Instead, it was to be for one which was closely based on assets of all sorts and on ability to pay. Why was such a broadly-based reassessment needed? William's scorched-earth policy had made arbitrary reductions necessary; but recoveries had been made since. Domesday Book shows that a very recent reassessment of land had begun in the south-eastern counties, but it led to lower assessments not higher. In 1084 geld at the high rate of six shillings (30p) had already been levied, but incompletely collected. Because of this the men who had accompanied William and become powerful magnates knew that their successful take-over bid was in jeopardy.

To face the 200 ships assembled by the Danish king in 1084 William had brought over to this country a 'larger force of soldiers and mounted men than had ever come to this country before'. He had now to accommodate them with his magnates 'each in proportion to their land'. Yet many of the wealthiest lands lay untapped and exempt. I would argue that the main item in Domesday Book which has not yet found an accepted definition – the ploughland or teamland – represents a new effort at fiscal reappraisal. It was based on variable assets in different regions, but essentially upon arable land and its ancillary assets, such as meadow for the plough-teams. Several chroniclers put plough-teams at the head of their list of items the Domesday Inquiry sought; and several associate the inquiry with taxation. Indeed, the recent statistical work of Mcdonald and Snooks demonstrates that the existing assessment of Essex shows a relatively much higher incidence of taxation on the smallest holdings (see Figure 2). If taxation were to be increased it could only be achieved by tying its incidence accurately to resources.

To summarise: the aims of the Domesday Inquiry were threefold. It checked tenure, it valued lands for the levy of feudal aids, and it recorded assets for a basic fiscal reassessment; all spheres of interest for the twelfth-century Exchequer. These aims were precise and within the limits of any great questionnaire, almost completely fulfilled. The construc-

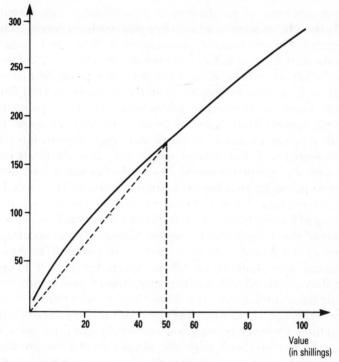

Tax
(Assessment in acres)

Value
(in shillings)

Figure 2 The tax assessment–manorial annual value relationship for
Essex lay-manors 1086

From J. Mcdonald and G. D. Snooks, 'How Artificial were the Tax
Assessments of Domesday England? The Case of Essex', *Ec. Hist. Rev.*
(1985).

tion of Domesday Book enforced a great welding of Anglo-
Saxon practices and Norman feudal interests, in which the
growth of the Exchequer was securely rooted. There was also
a direct result. All landholders of consequence were sum-
moned to Salisbury in 1086 to take an oath of fealty to William
'no matter whose vassals they might be.' It tied both great
magnates and powerful under-tenants to the king on the basis
of the full-scale data for feudal obligations and fiscal dues
contained in Domesday Book.

57

Reconstruction of pre-Conquest landholdings has recently thrown light on some continuity of practice from Anglo-Saxon England. On the basis of an analysis of these pre-Conquest landholders Sawyer has questioned the existence of a 'tenurial revolution' at the time of the Conquest. Accepting the massive change in *persons* he argues that the *structures* of post-Conquest lordships frequently followed in the footsteps of the pre-Conquest. That Norman lords were often assigned the lands in several counties of particular Anglo-Saxons has long been recognised, but Sawyer emphasises that the lands held by men and women *commended* to an Anglo-Saxon lord, were also acquired by that lord's Norman successor, then given to his sub-tenants. Thus, the tenurial change was not usually a matter of a small group of powerful newcomers taking over the lands of many small pre-Conquest 'thegns'. Great accumulations of land and influence had been common in Saxon England also. Gilbert de Ghent succeeded to Ulf Fenisc, Geoffrey de Mandeville to Asgar the Staller, and Count Alan of Brittany to Eadgifu the Fair. Yet, it is doubtful if the proportion of continuity and discontinuity of landholding structures can ever be weighed accurately given the data we have. Domesday Book does not usually record the pre-Conquest holder and, even when it does, it is not always possible to identify him with certainty unless a second name or title is given. Also, the characteristics of the two types of lordship remained different. However, it is worth noting that, in addition to the earls, there was a small group of very powerful landholders in Anglo-Saxon England, just as in Norman England.

The links between the two power structures and the close similarity of status between Anglo-Saxon and Norman sheriffs has now also been highlighted. Continuity amongst the class of skilled royal functionaries such as goldsmiths, foresters, or huntsmen has always been visible clearly in Domesday Book. Other strands of continuity have recently been emphasised. Eleanor Searle has shown how marriages between the new landholders and the daughters or widows of Anglo-Saxon landholders helped to give a smooth transfer, a legitimacy and, arguably, a respect for the new regime. This was important if the new lords were ever to be acceptable and safe. It embodied a change of legal principles and a nice use of them. Women could anyway hold and transfer land in their own right in the Anglo-Saxon period. Under the Norman law they could not. But they could still be the means of its transfer as heiresses and widows. Hence the king's – and his barons' – consent was needed for the marriage of heiresses. This was an important factor in the rebellion and repercussions following the marriage in 1075 between the daughter of Ralf of East Anglia and the Earl of Hereford for which consent had been refused. Only two Englishmen of importance retained their lands in Domesday; one, Colswein of Lincoln, left only a daughter who was married to a Norman, whilst Turchil of Warwick's lands may have descended with his daughter and her marriage. Finally, a sector of the Anglo-Saxon ecclesiastical landholding world has been given a new lease of life. Blair has shown that secular ministers were not ousted by Benedictine monasteries in the early Norman period. On the contrary they continued to have strong influence.

WEALTH AND TAXES

The extraordinary range and detail of Domesday Book means that, even 200 years after publication, there is still further information to be gained from the use of its data.

Steady progress has been made by Darby in transforming Domesday data into maps in five regional volumes of Domesday geographies, together with a gazetteer volume which also maps Domesday settlements. The series was completed by a final volume in 1977 on Domesday England as a whole. Maps now make assimilable the basic items in Domesday, the most fundamental to the economy being the distribution of population. Though the adult rural male population was recorded, the figures in Domesday, mapped by Darby, are minima. The households of baronial and manorial lords were not recorded. Nor were all the towns included, and of those that were, the classes of population were often incomplete. Population distribution also makes clear where much of the weight of the economy lay. The heaviest concentrations were in the counties of East Anglia and Essex, and on the Kent and Sussex coastlines. In central and southern England, south of a line from the Humber to the Severn estuary, population was well distributed. North of this line it was sparse in many areas.

In Darby's maps of waste (previously cultivated land of little or no value when the survey was taken) it is now easy to see both the devastation present at the end of the Confessor's reign, and that resulting from the Conqueror's subjugation of the north and west. The balance of the economy was certainly affected by this throughout the Conqueror's reign and beyond. The devastation of the city of York on two occasions, together with the wasting of its hinterland, is in marked contrast to the increased traffic of London, Dover, Winchester and Wight to Normandy and Flanders. This reinforced the high levels of population, and the already extensive agricultural exploitation of eastern England and parts of the south coast. The portrayal by Le Patourel of the Norman advent as waves of colonisation of the British Isles northwards and westwards, not as a single conquest, accords with this economic picture. Despite all the exertions of William's military strength in the north, Domesday surveys only south Lancashire (between the Ribble and the Mersey), and Yorkshire – and no further.

On how wealth was generated, Domesday information in general, and the annual values in particular, still have much to tell us. Although Galbraith put the annual values of land at the centre of the Inquiry he himself dismissed them as often 'manifestly bogus'; and Darby did not map them until near the conclusion of his great geographies. Only recently have they been given the attention they deserve. The values were shown by Harvey to have been used by contemporaries in their transactions; their validity has been confirmed by Mcdonald and Snooks in a recent statistical computer study of Essex – the county with the most detailed information. They demonstrated that the values were closely allied to assets and manpower, and therefore were realistic.

The values – the net income of lands to king and landholders – represent the surplus over subsistence generated in the countryside, and show England to have been a wealthy

What is the name of the manor?
Who held it in the time of King Edward?
Who holds it now?
How many hides are there?
How many teams – in demesne – of the tenants?
How many villeins – cottars – slaves?
How many freemen – sokemen?
How much wood – meadow – pasture?
How many mills – fisheries?
How much has been added or taken away?
How much was the whole worth? How much now?
How much had or has each freeman sokeman?
All this to be given thrice; that is, in the time of King
Edward, when King William gave it, and at the present
time.
And, if more can be had than is had?
[From the *Inquest of Ely*]

Illustration 2   Questions asked in the Domesday Inquiry

state. The considerable agrarian-based surplus helps to explain how England was able repeatedly to raise large sums in
taxation, much of which, before and after the Norman Conquest, left the country.

How was this surplus achieved? Sawyer suggested that the
silver for the large quantity of silver coin raised in taxation
was obtained via the export of wool and sheepskins to the
Flemish cloth industry. Exeter Domesday and Little Domesday, for the south-west and eastern England, show large
numbers of sheep kept on 'demesnes'. The total, including the
unrecorded flocks of freeholders, villeins, and smallholders,
might well have been considerable. But Mcdonald and
Snooks's statistical analysis on values in Essex, questions the
role of livestock in producing significant profits. They argue,
from a high degree of correlation between the working ploughs
and the values, that incomes from land were largely based
upon arable. However, the sample of Essex lay landholders is
too small geographically, and covers only a part of the range
of landlord choices and structures. Other counties need similar

studies to resolve this important difference in interpretation.

Other interesting questions about the varied economic preferences and organisation of different landholders are now being asked. From the detailed Essex computer analysis it has been concluded that on the lay estates there was little difference in agricultural methods. This can be compared with the results of a simple country-wide analysis by Harvey of the structure of estates, based upon the plough-teams of the demesne, and the plough-teams of the villeins and tenants. The great demesnes mostly belonged to the monastic houses, and only a mere handful of the great lay landlords were interested in demesne agriculture. Demesne agriculture needed a large work-force and a number of supervisory staff, such as reeves and riding-men; and there were close links between demesne agriculture and slavery. (The absence of slavery in much of eastern England and the rapid decline of slavery under the Normans is a notable feature of Domesday England.) In contrast, leading lay lords with large manors went for the easier profits available from raising rents and transforming former small dues into full-scale rents: a policy facilitated by the political circumstances of the Conquest. From these studies we can see that there was in fact quite a range of landlord choices and structures.

How far these profits from landholding were successfully tapped by fiscal levies, and how up to date were the assessments, is another important area of enquiry. As we have seen, a study of Essex (see Figure 2), indicates that tax was regressive, with the tax rate declining relatively as the value of the holding increased. Thus, both the economic and the fiscal evidence points to the small producer as providing an increasing proportion of England's disposable wealth.

It is evident, therefore, that modern research on Domesday Book has resulted in some important changes in historical interpretation. It has revealed: that Domesday Book served a diversity of purposes; that there were substantial continuities between Anglo-Saxon and Norman England; that Domesday England possessed great wealth; and that the tax system was an efficient means of exploiting that wealth, particularly in relation to the small producer.

REFERENCES AND FURTHER READING

(1) **R. Welldon Finn,** *An Introduction to Domesday Book* (London, 1986).
(2) **V. H. Galbraith,** *Domesday Book: its Place in Administrative History* (Oxford, 1974).
(3) **H. C. Darby,** *Domesday England* (Cambridge, 1986).
(4) **P. Sawyer** (ed.), *Domesday Book: A Reassessment* (London, 1985).
(5) **S. Harvey,** 'Domesday England' in *The Agrarian History of England and Wales,* 11 (Cambridge, 1987).
(6) **S. Harvey,** *Domesday Book and its Purpose* (London, 1987).
(7) **J. Mcdonald and G. D. Snooks,** 'How Artificial were the Tax Assessments of Domesday England? The Case of Essex', *Economic History Review,* 2nd series, xxxviii (1985).

5 The Industrial Revolution: Economic Growth in Britain, 1700–1860

N. F. R. CRAFTS

The publication in 1962 of Deane and Cole's *British Economic Growth* [2] was of major significance to the economic history of the first industrial revolution. It offered new estimates of the overall rate of economic growth, and of changes in the structure of economic activity. These in turn provided a context for fresh investigation of a range of subjects of central importance, including the growth of individual industries, foreign trade, population change, crop yields and living standards.

NEW APPROACHES

The fact that their work enabled scholars to quantify the structure changes in the economy also influenced critical aspects of the *concept* itself. By the 1960s this had normally come to be defined in terms of overall changes in the sectoral structure of the economy. For example, this approach was adopted in the classic study by David Landes [4], when he defined the industrial revolution in Britain as 'the first historical instance of the breakthrough from an agrarian, handicraft economy to one dominated by industry and machine manufacture'.

Much of the early use and discussion of Deane and Cole's work was related to the famous 'stages' theory of economic growth advanced in 1960 by Rostow [5], who put forward the proposition that the British economy had experienced a

64

'take-off into self-sustained growth' in the period 1783–1802. He saw the take-off as a 'decisive transition' involving sharp rises in the share of the country's resources allocated to investment, and the emergence of leading sectors (cotton and iron), which exerted a powerful influence over growth as a whole. Rostow also suggested that this British experience was the prototype for all other industrialised countries.

Deane and Cole's estimates did not give much support to Rostow's hypotheses. They suggested a much more gradualist interpretation of overall growth as backdrop to the dramatic, but not dominant, developments in cotton and iron production; and they indicated that the rise in investment had been quite modest relative to the increase in total output. This part of Deane and Cole's work was quickly adopted in the best introductory texts. For example, Flinn [3] sums up as follows: '. . . the lesson to be learnt from the statistics appears to be one of the superimposition upon a steadily growing economy of a small group of extremely dynamic sectors. Statistically they represented, even by the end of the century, a very small share of the national product, but the growth in them was sufficient to double the existing rate of overall growth in the economy.'

Subsequent work has refined and extended further aspects of Deane and Cole's pioneering study. Further studies have improved their original data-base; and estimates for other European countries have allowed Britain's experience to be studied in an international perspective. The implications for the growth of output per worker, and of agriculture's contribution to the process of industrialisation have been discussed in quantitative terms. Most recently, Crafts [1] has attempted to bring together the various strands in the literature, and to offer a new synthesis to measure, describe and explain British economic growth during the industrial revolution. As a result of this new work the Rostovian picture of a dramatic take-off has been decisively rejected, and the present evidence supports a more gradualist interpretation of the industrial revolution.

RESULTS OF RECENT RESEARCH

Crafts's new estimates of economic growth are presented in

65

Table 4, together with those made earlier by Deane and Cole. It must be borne in mind that the underlying data for this period will never permit precise and definitive statements. The most that can be done is to make careful 'guesstimates' in the light of both the available sources and general economic and statistical reasoning.

Crafts's estimates thus build on the work of Deane and Cole and of many other scholars who have researched in this area in the past decade. To a large extent they rely on the same original sources such as tax returns and customs and excise records. The recent improvements in knowledge have come primarily not from new sources of information but from the application of more sophisticated methods of data analysis. Examples of this in the demographic sphere are given in Chapter 8.

Table 4   Growth rates of real output, 1700–1860 (per cent per year)

	Industrial Output		Whole Economy (GDP)	
	Crafts	*Deane and Cole*	*Crafts*	*Deane and Cole*
	(1)	(2)	(3)	(4)
1700–1760	0.7	1.0	0.7	0.7
1760–1780	1.5	0.5	0.7	0.6
1780–1801	2.1	3.4	1.3	2.1
1801–1831	3.0	4.4	2.0	3.1
1831–1860	3.3	3.0	2.5	2.2

Source: Cols (1) and (3): Crafts [1], pp. 32, 45, 81 and 84. (2) and (4): Deane and Cole [2], pp. 78, 166 and 170.
Note: Figures for 1700–1801 are for England and Wales, thereafter for Great Britain.

The new estimates of the growth of industrial output between 1780 and 1830 show substantially lower rates of increase in most periods (compare columns 1 and 2 of Table 4). The differences are particularly large in the 'classic' period of the industrial revolution, 1780–1830. From 1780 to 1801 the old estimate of 3.4 per cent per year is reduced to only 2.1 per cent per year, and for 1801–31 the rate is cut sharply from

4.4 to 3.0 per cent per year. The same is true for growth in the economy as a whole, including agriculture and services (see columns 3 and 4 of Table 4). The picture which now emerges is thus one of steady growth, rather than a 'take-off' or spectacular acceleration.

It is true that growth in a few very dynamic industries was very rapid, and far outstripped the expansion of industrial output as a whole. Thus the production of cotton textiles grew at a rate of 9.7 per cent per year from 1780 to 1801, and of 5.6 per cent per year from 1801 to 1831. Iron production grew at rates of 5.1 and 4.6 per cent per year over the same periods. However, even by 1831 cotton accounted for little more than a fifth of total industrial output, and iron for less than one-tenth. Much of 'industry' was still composed of traditional, handicraft activity. Even by 1831 only about one in ten of all workers was employed in the modern 'manufacturing' sector of the economy, compared with almost three times as many working in other forms of industry.

INVESTMENT AND PRODUCTIVITY

We also have new information about the factors of production employed to manufacture this output. There are new series for the growth of the labour force; for the level of capital investment (i.e. of spending on the construction or purchase of long-lasting productive assets such as machinery, mills, mines, warehouses, canals and ships); and about the total stock of such fixed capital built up over time. These series can be combined with the revised output estimates in order to analyse how this expansion of output was achieved. In particular, we can ask to what extent increased output was obtained simply by using more labour and capital, and to what extent by greater efficiency in use of these resources. The latter result might, for example, be achieved by getting more output from an unchanged level of labour and capital inputs. The name given to this measure of the relationship between output and the use of all inputs combined is *total factor productivity* (see the box).

A first step towards answering these questions is taken in

Table 5. This shows the trend over time in the investment ratio, i.e. in the proportion of the country's national income allocated to acquisition of long-lasting capital assets which could be used to produce future goods and services, rather than to current consumption, government expenditure (mainly on wars) or net exports. We see that the proportion devoted to investment did increase over time – from about 7 per cent at the end of the eighteenth century to over 11 per cent in 1831–60; and by that period the British economy was adding to its stock of capital assets at a rate which was extremely high by the standard of any previous period. But there was no take-off, no period in which there was a sudden acceleration in the investment ratio.

Table 5   Investment as a percentage of national income, 1700–1860

1700–1760	5.0
1760–1800	7.0
1801–1831	10.0
1831–1860	11.3

Source: Crafts [1], p. 81.

The second and more direct step towards an answer to our question about the sources of economic growth is taken in Table 6. This shows the rate of growth of labour and capital in columns (1) and (2), and combines them to get a measure of the growth of total factor inputs in column (3). The rate of growth of output is shown in column (4), and the difference between output and inputs represents the growth of total factor productivity. A consequence of the downward revisions to the growth estimates noted above is that the rate of growth of total factor productivity (column 5) now appears markedly lower than previous writers believed. Once again the notion of a spectacular 'take-off' is rejected by the evidence now available. Nevertheless, it should be appreciated that by the second quarter of the nineteenth century the economy had achieved a rate of growth of total factor productivity which would previously have been inconceivable: as column (5) of Table 6 shows the rate had accelerated from 0.3 per cent per year to 1.0 per cent per year.

Table 6   Sources of economic growth, 1700–1860
(Growth rates, per cent, per year)

	Capital Stock (1)	Labour Force (2)	Total Factor Inputs (3)	Output (GDP) (4)	Total Factor Productivity (5)
1700–1760	0.7	0.3	0.4	0.7	0.3
1760–1800	1.0	0.8	0.8	1.0	0.2
1801–1831	1.5	1.4	1.3	2.0	0.7
1831–1860	2.0	1.4	1.5	2.5	1.0

Source: Crafts [1], p. 81.

Note: Land is not shown separately, but is included in col. (3).

These were important developments which eventually allowed the famous 'Malthusian' threat to living standards from rising population to be overcome. Prior to about 1830, however, the growth of total real output did not exceed population growth by much, and real wages were growing at only a little over 0.5 per cent per year.

With the idea of an industrial revolution in mind it is also interesting to delve a little further into the growth of output per worker (labour productivity) in different parts of the economy. A tentative classification suggests the following. First, the growth of productivity in agriculture was somewhat faster than that in industry. Second, within industry were to be found the few sectors where productivity growth was really fast; most notably in textiles, with its radical changes in technology. But alongside these famous industries were a large set of traditional activities, including building, and the food, brewing and leather industries, where there was virtually no advance in productivity.

STRUCTURAL CHANGE

Changes in the structure of output and employment are the focus of Table 7 which relates directly to the notion of the industrial revolution mentioned above as defined, for example, by Landes [4]. This table reports not only the results of recent research on Britain but also permits comparison with European experience. The 'European norms' shown in the table can be thought of as a measure of the average experience of Western European countries at the point in time when they eventually reached the level of income per head which Britain had attained in the year stated. Take, for example, the figures for 1840 in rows 1 and 2: row 1 says that in 1840 Britain had 47.3 per cent of its male labour force in industry. Row 2 tells us that the corresponding proportion for the European countries – calculated at the dates at which each subsequently reached the per capita income level which Britain had enjoyed in 1840 – averaged only 25.3 per cent.

Table 7   A comparison of British and European changes in economic structure 1700–1840 (percentages)

	1700	1760	1840
Male labour force			
In Industry			
1 Britain	18.5	23.8	47.3
2 European norm	12.6	16.9	25.3
In Agriculture			
3 Britain	61.2	52.8	28.6
4 European norm	72.0	66.2	54.9
Output			
In Industry			
5 Britain	20.0	20.0	31.5
6 European norm	19.3	21.3	25.2
In Primary sector			
7 Britain	37.4	37.5	24.9
8 European norm	51.4	46.6	37.2
Urbanisation			
% of population			
9 Britain	. .	. .	48.4
10 European norm	. .	. .	31.4

Source: Crafts [1], pp. 62–3.

Note: The labour force estimates in rows 1–4 are for principal employment. The primary sector in rows 7–8 covers extractive industry as well as agriculture.

Table 7 reflects the enormous change in economic structure in Britain between 1760 and 1840: the expansion of the share of labour and output devoted to industry (rows 1 and 5), and the decline of the share of agriculture (rows 3 and 7). It also shows vividly how different this transformation was from the general European experience. The British economy in 1840 had a much lower proportion of its labour force in agriculture than the European countries at the corresponding stage in their development (28.6 against 54.9 per cent), but a much higher degree of industrialisation (compare rows 1 and 2, or 5 and 6) and of urbanisation (rows 9 and 10). Britain was *not the prototype* for other countries. They followed a different, less industrialised, path in their economic development.

THE KEY IMPLICATIONS

The term 'industrial revolution' is, of course, a metaphor and, as has long been recognised, it is in some ways a misleading one. The notion can now be more fully clarified in the light of the recent research summarised above.

(i) There was a revolutionary change in the structure of employment. In the late eighteenth and early nineteenth centuries the proportion of the labour force employed in industry increased, and the proportion employed in agriculture fell very rapidly.

(ii) Much of the employment in industry continued to be in small-scale, handicraft activities producing for local markets. These traditional industries were barely affected by technological advance, and so experienced little or no increase in output per worker.

(iii) The acceleration in the overall pace of economic growth was perceptible, but relatively modest. There was no great leap forward for the economy as a whole, or even for the whole of industry, despite the spectacular growth of cotton textile production.

(iv) The rate of economic growth increased as more was invested in fixed capital, and productivity growth quickened. There were deservedly famous technological advances such as Crompton's mule and Watt's steam engine. These developments aided Britain's exports of manufacturers. However, in most of the economy, productivity growth remained painfully slow in the first half of the nineteenth century.

(v) Mid-nineteenth-century Britain is often labelled the 'workshop of the world', and the advance of productivity in a few industries did indeed enable Britain to sell around half of all world trade in manufactures. However, this should not blind one to the key implication of Tables 6 and 7: the main feature of British industrialisation involved getting a lot of workers into the industrial sector, not getting a high level of output per worker from them once they were there. Co-existing with the cotton and the other famous export sectors were many low productivity, low-paid and non-exporting industries.

THE ROLE OF AGRICULTURE

The unusually low share of employment in agriculture in Britain (as compared to Europe) by the early nineteenth century prompts the question: how did this happen? At one level it is quite easy to explain. By international standards labour productivity in British agriculture was very high (in 1840, for example, output per worker in French agriculture was only about 60 per cent of the British level), and it had grown significantly from the sixteenth century on. From 1750 to 1850 the number of jobs in agriculture rose only very slowly, while the number of non-farm workers who could be fed by the output of each farm worker rose more than 2.5 times. Productivity increases were achieved by better crop yields from rotations involving legumes and fodder crops, by increases in farm size and by investment in livestock, drainage and implements. (For further discussion of these and related changes in agriculture see Chapters 1 and 2.) As a result of these advances in agricultural techniques during the period of the industrial revolution, the growth in total factor productivity in the economy as a whole exceeded that in the industrial sector, though not that in factory industry alone. These important agricultural improvements after 1750 should always be remembered so that the phrase 'industrial revolution' does not mislead.

Productivity is the term used for the relationship between output and one or more of the factors of production (land, labour, capital). Changes over time tell us about changes in the efficiency with which the factors are used to produce goods and services. The most common use of the term is in relation to *labour productivity*, which measures the change in output per worker. Another familiar measure is the *productivity of land*, for example of farm output per acre. Both of these measure efficiency in relation to a single factor. In the case of labour productivity this means that we have no way of judging how much of any increase is the result of, say, harder work on the part of the labour force, and how much is the result of more capital equipment. To get round this problem it is necessary to find a way to measure the growth of the combined inputs of land, labour and capital, and when this is done we can measure changes in the efficiency of all inputs taken together. This is called *total factor productivity*.

At the same time the very success of agriculture makes its declining relative importance a bit puzzling. If we were so good at farming why did we come to rely so much on imported food (over a fifth of our consumption by 1840)? This problem has only recently begun to receive serious attention, and the answer is not yet fully understood. It seems likely that one reason is to be found in Britain's even greater superiority in producing textiles for export. (This phenomenon was bad news for farmers in the same way that North Sea oil exports over the past decade have paid for imports of manufactured goods at the expense of domestic manufacturing.) Another possible reason is the strong impact of income growth on the demand for services and handicrafts in both town and country.

STANDARDS OF LIVING

The impact of early industrialisation on workers' living standards has, of course, long been controversial. The view of economic growth presented above offers some useful perspectives on this debate. The new, lower, estimates of growth in the economy as a whole suggest that the slow growth of real wages came from low productivity growth and very modest increases in the amount of capital equipment per worker, rather than from a massive increase in profits at the expense of wages, as had seemed possible on Deane and Cole's evidence. Over the period 1780–1850 real wages and real national income per head probably grew at the same rate [Crafts (1) p. 103].

The finding that relatively little employment initially was in sectors experiencing rapid productivity growth also has important implications for the distribution of the gains from economic growth. The modernised sectors were concentrated in the North of England, where wage rates became much higher than in the South. This differential was not eliminated by internal migration. It is *possible* that a majority of workers experienced no gain in real earnings before the 1830s [Crafts (1) pp. 105–6], but much more research is needed on the regional details of prices and wages before this can be verified.

However, since economic growth is now seen to be slower than was previously thought, the effect of changes in the *quality of life* assumes a particularly important part in questions of movements in living standards; and the new estimates do not shed any light on these developments. Whilst not all such changes were for the worse – for example, life expectancy as a whole increased – many adverse factors did come into play. These included reductions in leisure time, deterioration in the environment, and, arguably, new forms of class relationship.

LATER ECONOMIC PERFORMANCE

The picture of economic growth during the industrial revolution sketched above can be elaborated to make greater sense of Britain's relative decline later on in the nineteenth century. It is certainly true that Britain in 1850 had the highest income level in the world, and accounted for perhaps a third of total world industrial production. Nevertheless, some aspects of our development to that point were not impressive and did not hold out promise of subsequent rapid growth.

74

*Our exports were dominated by textiles, and increasingly sold to the low-income countries rather than to those already industrialised.

*Productivity advance was not spectacular across the economy as a whole. Equally importantly, it was based neither on research and development investment, nor on investment in education, and it was thus unlike the advances in productivity to come after 1880 [Crafts (1) ch. 8].

*The development of the economy before 1860 was based neither on very high levels of home investment, nor on modern financial institutions. As a result, the capital market was ill-suited to ensuring an efficient use of investible funds.

*Finally, by the mid-nineteenth century Britain's early start and considerable wealth led naturally to the development of a substantial stream of investment abroad, reaching around 5 per cent of national income by the end of the 1860s. The profits from this foreign investment perhaps inhibited subsequent investment in home manufacturing through their effects on the balance of external payments [Crafts (1) p. 163].

While it is useful to see how many of the roots of Britain's problems in the late nineteenth century reach back to the pattern of development in the earlier period, this does not detract from the importance of the first industrial revolution. Even if we now believe that it proceeded at a relatively modest pace, and that the really revolutionary changes were for long confined to a limited part of the whole economy, it remains true that Britain had brought about a remarkable transformation in the way a society provided itself with material goods. This will always be seen as an event of the greatest historical significance.

REFERENCES AND FURTHER READING

(1) **N. F. R. Crafts,** *British Economic Growth during the Industrial Revolution* (Oxford, 1985).
(2) **P. M. Deane and W. A. Cole,** *British Economic Growth, 1688–1959* (Cambridge, 1962).
(3) **M. W. Flinn,** *Origins of the Industrial Revolution* (London, 1966).
(4) **D. S. Landes,** *The Unbound Prometheus* (Cambridge, 1969).
(5) **W. W. Rostow,** *The Stages of Economic Growth* (Cambridge, 1960).

6 British Imperialism: a Review and a Revision

A. G. HOPKINS

'How is the Empire?' George V's last words, spoken in 1936, voiced a preoccupation of monarchs and governments which sounded across three centuries of British history. Even today, there is a sense in which the empire lives on. Its presence is felt in the imperial legacies of the Commonwealth – from the heights of the English language to the depths of the malfunctioning colonial telephone. In 1988, no less than in 1688, the need for security and the quest for wealth continue to draw Britain into the wider world, and policy-makers still strive, as they have for generations, to ensure that they do not preside over 'an insignificant island in the North Sea'.

The importance of the empire has long since elevated its study to the status of a specialisation. This badge of academic rank has encouraged historical research of wide range and deep erudition. The causes of empire-building, the means by which the empire was controlled, and the consequences of the 'imperial experience' are subjects which have generated a literature so substantial as to make even bibliographers blanch [Cain (2), Louis (8), Owen and Sutcliffe (10), Davies and Huttenback (5), Hopkins (7)]. This formidable academic advance has also erected barriers to non-specialists, who are understandably uncertain of the terms and contours of debate. Indeed, specialisation has ensured that the study of imperialism and empire has been very largely disconnected from what is conventionally regarded as forming the 'mainstream' of British economic and social history. The purpose of this chapter is to suggest that neither the empire nor the metropolis can be understood in isolation, and that integrating them

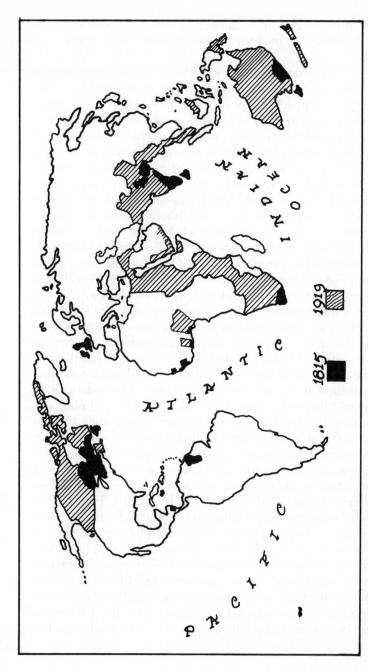

Map 4 The growth of the British Empire was depicted in most contemporary studies by maps. The map projection was chosen carefully to maximise the extent of British territory, and this effect was enhanced, where possible, by colouring the map an imperial red.

alters our perception of themes which are central to an understanding of modern British history – at home and abroad.

There was a time when the study of imperial history lacked the complications introduced by modern scholarship. The empire was defined by the constitutional status of its parts, which were coloured red on the map of the world (see Map 4). Its history took the form of a political narrative animated by white heroes who symbolised the adventurous and progressive spirit of the age, whether Tudor or Victorian. This perspective was particularly congenial to the advocates of empire who promoted it. But it came under powerful attack in the late nineteenth century from dissenting liberals, such as Hobson, and from a clutch of radical and Marxist writers, whose hostile accounts of the causes and consequences of imperialism culminated in Lenin's analysis of the relationship between colonial rivalries and the outbreak of the First World War [Brewer (1), Owen and Sutcliffe (10)]. The alternative interpretation advanced by these commentators is conventionally referred to as the theory of economic imperialism, though recent research has revealed that there were several theories aimed at different targets. However, it remains true that the leading critics based their analysis of empire-building on what they presumed to be the central laws or tendencies of advanced industrial societies. Hence they emphasised, variously, the development of 'finance capitalism', the rise of cartels and monopolies, and the political influence of the industrial bourgeoisie, and they regarded imperialism as being an external expression of these novel domestic forces.

The Marxist thesis provoked a liberal reaction which introduced a new set of complexities [Cain (2)]. Flaws in the theory of economic imperialism were revealed, and attempts were made to restate orthodox approaches by presenting them in a more scholarly and less partisan way. Emphasis was placed on multicausal explanations which explored various non-economic considerations and underlined the role of individuals, coincidence and chance. Some scholars stressed the importance of international diplomacy and the balance of power; others explored the ideological and racial impulses behind imperialism; still others examined the role of national-ism and forms of 'social imperialism' linked to urbanisation, wage-employment, and democracy.

This counter-revolution culminated in the work of Gal-lagher and Robinson in the 1950s and 60s [Louis (8), Robin-son and Gallagher (9)]. Gallagher and Robinson managed to escape from the traditional political framework which shackled orthodox studies of the empire while also avoiding the notion that the late nineteenth century was characterised by a form of 'new imperialism' arising out of an advanced stage of industrial capitalism. They drew attention instead to the underlying continuities of British imperialism. The indus-trial revolution had created the conditions for successful overseas expansion from an early point in the nineteenth century. Britain was indeed an expanding power. But for much of the period she was able to spread *informally*, by exercising commercial, cultural and diplomatic influence, whereas in the last quarter of the century new territories, principally in Africa, were incorporated into the *formal* empire. The underlying aim, British supremacy, remained constant. It was the means, not the motive, which changed. This happened not because industrial capitalism entered a novel phase but because Britain was harassed by foreign rivals (principally France and Germany) and plagued by a string of crises on distant peripheries. A final elaboration, Robinson's 'excentric' theory of imperialism, shifted the explanation even further from the metropolis and made the colonised collabor-ators in their own subordination [Owen and Sutcliffe (10)]. By redefining the concept of empire, Gallagher and Robinson were able to offer a coherent and illuminating account which made Marxist interpretation of nineteenth-century imperial-ism appear dated and, in the eyes of some writers, redundant too.

Curiously, Marxist historians were slow to respond to this challenge. They were sceptical, in principle, of bourgeois research (a feeling that was fully reciprocated by liberal scholars), and they adhered to stereotyped generalisations about the evolution of industrial capitalism and the drive to empire. A thorough Marxist account of the partition of Africa, based on the detailed research now available, has still to be written. However, Gallagher and Robinson's thesis did provoke substantial comment and criticism from non-Marxist quarters during the 1960s and 70s. Some scholars cast doubt on the claim that Britain had established an informal 'empire' in the mid-nineteenth century; others revealed serious weaknesses in their interpretation of the partition of Africa [Louis (8), Hopkins (6)]. Case studies reflecting a new sensitivity towards the history of the Third World multiplied, and the subject began to show pronounced centrifugal tendencies.

Historians seeking to understand this topic now face a difficult choice. Traditional, Marxist-style theories of imperialism are appealingly comprehensive but run into conceptual and empirical difficulties. Non-Marxist interpretations are likely to reflect the results of recent research, but incline to fragment under a weight of detail. To conclude that 'the truth lies somewhere between two extremes', is vaguely judicious, but it avoids saying why this should be the case or where the point of balance lies, and so consigns us to the place occupied by those who, as Burke put it, are 'resolved to die in the last dyke of prevarication'.

The remainder of this essay will sketch a way out of this dilemma [Cain and Hopkins (3, 4)]. The presentation will necessarily be brief, but the absence of qualification is not to be taken as a sign that the reader is being offered the final solution to the riddle of the ages. The aim is rather to open up a line of enquiry which is intended to be a constructive and modestly interesting contribution to a long-running and important debate.

The point of departure lies in questioning the central assumption, accepted by Marxist and non-Marxist writers alike, that British imperialism in the nineteenth century was essentially a product of the industrial revolution. Recent research suggests an alternative way of shaping British economic and social history during this period. Of course, industrialisation was of central importance; but it is now clear that it was also a more protracted and fragmented process than was once thought. Moreover, the rise of industry needs to be set in the context of a broader pattern of economic development which began in London in the late seventeenth century, expanded during the classic phase of industrialisation in the nineteenth century, and continued to grow in south-east England in the twentieth century, when Britain's position as an industrial power entered a period of relative decline. This pattern of modernisation was created by a revolution in finance and commercial services which found expression in the foundation of the Bank of England, the establishment of the national debt, the rise of the stock exchange and of the major insurance companies, and in a cluster of commercial innovations which helped to give Britain a competitive edge in international trade.

These were progressive, profit-seeking activities which can properly be called capitalist. But their capitalist qualities were of a particular kind, being associated with managing men and money rather than machines, and being removed from direct contact with the world of manufacturing in the midlands and the north. They pointed the way forward to an economic order which remains easily recognisable today, but they also proved to be compatible with the existing social hierarchy, and thus enabled change to be combined with stability. The leading representatives of the City and the service sector in the south-east not only made large fortunes but made them in ways which were socially acceptable: they were gentlemen as well as capitalists. This unusually favourable blend of economic and cultural attributes also conferred political privileges. Unlike their counterparts in industry, bankers and merchants in the City were able to use their geographical location and social ties to make valuable political connections in the capital, and they had the leisure necessary to cultivate them too.

The notion of gentlemanly capitalism is intended to give direction to the argument without imposing a strait-jacket on the past. Gentlemen-capitalists are not to be seen as ingredients in a new conspiracy theory, for they were close to the structure of authority (where they were not already part of it), and their views were openly canvassed. Recognising the links between economy, society, and political life avoids determinism; identifying specific phases in the evolution of the gentlemanly capitalist order counters excessive generality.

Two broad phases (each with its own undulations) can be

distinguished. The period between 1688 and 1850 was dominated by an alliance of established landowners and new 'monied men', who defended the Glorious Revolution, profited from the patronage system and the national debt, and underwrote political stability. As the eighteenth century advanced, this structure experienced increasing budgetary and political difficulties, at home and abroad, and after 1815 reforms were introduced which curtailed patronage, installed 'Gladstonian finance', and dismantled protectionism. By the middle of the nineteenth century, the transition to a 'leaner, fitter Britain' was complete. Thereafter, during the second phase, the importance of landed power declined, and financial and service interests became the dominant elements in a realigned gentlemanly coalition which adapted, cautiously, to the dangerous world of democratic politics.

British imperialism can be seen as an attempt to shape a world system which both expressed and reinforced the gentlemanly order at home. In the eighteenth century this aim was achieved by a combination of conquest and protectionism; in the nineteenth century assertiveness was linked to the weapon of free trade, which was used to create openings for finance, commercial services and manufactures both within and beyond the established empire. The spread of sterling as the currency of world trade and the rapid growth of Britain's overseas investments after 1850 were the chief manifestations of this trend; the increasing dependence of the balance of payments on returns from foreign investment and from associated invisible earnings was one of its most striking consequences. Industry's needs were important; but the southern financial and service sector was the more dominant influence on Britain's presence abroad.

This interpretation can be illustrated by looking at the nineteenth century, the period which has generated the fiercest debate over the causes of British imperialism. The transition to 'responsible government' in the older, settled parts of the empire was designed to perpetuate Britain's interests in circumstances which no longer favoured protectionism or direction from the centre. As Disraeli observed in 1863: 'colonies do not cease to become colonies because they are independent'. What needs to be emphasised, however, is that

Britain's continuing influence in the dominions came to rest increasingly on exports of capital rather than on exports of manufactures. Canada (despite the influence of the United States) and Australia remained tied to London by their borrowing requirements, and, when necessary, they raised tariffs on British manufactures in order to balance their budgets and service external debts. India, which remained fully under Britain's control in the period before 1914, provided an even more striking example of the priority given to financial and service interests. The abolition of the East India Company's rule in 1858 symbolised the shift from the world of patronage and chartered companies to that populated by the new meritocratic class, drawn largely from southern England, who staffed the Indian Civil Service. These were men who equated good government with sound finance. British exporters undoubtedly gained greatly from the imposition of free trade on India, but their aspirations were limited by the imperatives of fiscal and monetary orthodoxy. In the longer term, the growth of investment in India was accompanied by a decline in the importance of the Lancashire lobby, a trend which culminated in the concession of tariff autonomy to India in 1917 and the loss of export markets in the subcontinent during the inter-war period.

The realignment of gentlemanly interests in Britain was also reflected in the additions made to the empire from the mid-nineteenth century. The acquisition of colonies in Africa was the most important of these extensions of empire, and it remains the most controversial. The interpretation advanced here suggests that Britain's participation in the 'scramble' for the continent can be considered along two axes: one, running from north to south, identifies expanding, and fiercely defended, financial commitments in Egypt and South Africa; the other, extending from west to east across tropical Africa, represents older manufacturing interests as well as (in east Africa) the appearance of a speculative financial element. This perspective enables the scramble for Africa to be viewed as a whole, while also emphasising the way in which sectoral differences in the development of the metropolitan economy found expression in diverse parts of the 'dark continent'.

Britain attempted to open a number of doors outside the

THE WHITE ELEPHANT
Present Proprietor (loq.). "SEE HERE GOVERNOR! HE'S A LIKELY-LOOKING ANIMAL—BUT *I*
CAN'T MANAGE HIM! IF *YOU* WON'T TAKE HIM, I MUST LET HIM GO!!"

Punch, October 22, 1892

Illustrations 3 and 4   The cartoons illustrate two of the fundamental themes
of imperialism. On the left, the 'Present Proprietor' (the Imperial British
East Africa Company), is asking the government to take over the economic
burden of maintaining imperial control over its African territory of Uganda.
On the right, the bond holder – behind the screen – is seen manipulating
the British government (represented by the prime minister, Lord Salisbury), and thus determining British foreign policy in the interests of those
who bought bonds and shares

empire too, but with limited results before the mid-nineteenth
century, despite Palmerston's forceful efforts in the 1830s and
40s. Thereafter, however, considerable success was achieved
in parts of south America, notably Argentina and Brazil,
where valuable markets for British capital and commercial
services were developed, and, with them, opportunities for
manufactured exports too. The extent to which these states
depended upon the flow of funds from Britain was demonstrated by the financial crises of the 1890s, which compelled

HOW LORD SALISBURY IS WORKED: A GLIMPSE BEHIND THE SCENE.

It is said that certain branches who have "dropped" millions on Turkish bonds are bringing the screw to bear on the Government so that they may recoup their loss.

Labour Leader, March 6, 1897

Argentina and Brazil to make domestic policy-adjustments to restore their external credit-worthiness. The governing elites of the two republics conformed to the 'rules of the game' because they admired British values as well as respected British power. The establishment of a branch of Harrods in Buenos Aires shortly before the First World War indicated just how completely the Argentine elite had accepted gentlemanly tastes.

Elsewhere, however, intentions were not matched by results. Bridgeheads were established in the Ottoman Empire and China, but advances were limited: neither the Ottomans nor the Manchus shopped at Harrods. Manufacturers wanted new customers, but could not secure government backing on

85

the scale required; governments were anxious to defend Britain's position in the Middle East and Far East, but were unable to compel the City to make investments which did not command the confidence of the market. The limits to British imperialism in these 'difficult' areas provided a measure of the City's privileged position in being independent of governments and in having an array of attractive alternatives. London could pick and choose; Paris and Berlin had to scramble for the fragments.

The older historiography which contrasted mid-Victorian quiescence with late-Victorian assertiveness is clearly misleading: Britain was undoubtedly an expanding, imperialist power in the nineteenth century. However, British imperialism was not a product of the 'inner logic' of industrial capitalism. Marx exaggerated the influence of the industrial bourgeoisie, and Marxists have overestimated the role of 'finance capital', as the term is normally understood, because connections between banks and industry were very limited before 1914. On the other hand, Gallagher and Robinson attach insufficient weight to structural changes in the economy during the nineteenth century, and consequently place too much emphasis on the degree of continuity in British imperialism. Britain's invisible 'empire' was more limited in the mid-nineteenth century than they suppose, and it grew rapidly after the 1870s, at precisely the time when they claim that it was in decline. Moreover, their emphasis on the periphery makes the tail wag the dog. There were numerous crises on many distant frontiers, but for the most part they were symptoms, not causes, of imperialism. These difficulties pose a problem; but the solution is not to be found in the machinations of foreign powers or in the argument, surely of last resort, that the empire was acquired 'in a fit of absence of mind'.

The interpretation advanced here suggests that the resolution of this dilemma lies in reappraising the contours of modern British economic and social history, and specifically in giving appropriate emphasis to developments which lay outside industry and remained largely independent of it. Imperialist impulses in the nineteenth century cannot be understood without placing the development of the financial and service sector – much neglected by economic historians as well as by specialists on imperialism – at the centre of the analysis, by tracing the growth of sterling as the motor of world commerce, and by exploring the ways in which wealth generated from overseas commerce helped to underpin the celebrated continuities of the British political system.

The scope for additional research is as wide as the argument itself. As far as British history is concerned, further thought needs to be given to the competitive and complementary features of the relationship between finance and manufacturing. On the periphery, the main interest lies in reappraising the role of external impulses as causes of local crises. Finally, by way of comparison, there is room for considering whether the argument developed here can be applied to other imperialist powers in Europe or whether, in the event, its main function is to underline the peculiarities of the English.

Britain's imperialist ambitions did not come to an end in 1914, despite a widespread view to the contrary. Strenuous attempts were made to recreate the pre-war international order in the 1920s, to forge a more manageable system based on the sterling area in the 1930s, and to strengthen imperial ties in the aftermath of the Second World War. The gentlemanly élite even succeeded in side-stepping the avalanche of decolonisation and in adjusting to the supremacy of the United States (and the dollar) during the 1950s and 60s. But a price had to be paid for keeping London at the centre of the world's financial markets. One view holds that the cost was borne by industry; another points to the threat posed to the autonomy of established City institutions by the intrusion of transnational corporations. From the perspective adopted in this essay, recent developments may have a deeper historical significance. The new Conservative policies imposed during the 1980s constitute a sustained and seemingly successful assault on the gentlemanly values of the liberal professions and occupations. Many of the old institutions and global aspirations remain; but the personnel have changed. Future historians may judge that the gentlemanly élite which held power from 1688 met its end in 1979, when Britain experienced another constitutional revolution: that of the *petit bourgeoisie*.

REFERENCES AND FURTHER READING

(1) **A. Brewer,** *Marxist Theories of Imperialism* (London, 1980).
(2) **P. J. Cain,** *Economic Foundations of British Overseas Expansion, 1815– 1914* (London, 1980).
(3) **P. J. Cain** and **A. G. Hopkins,** 'Gentlemanly Capitalism and British Expansion Overseas, I. The Old Colonial System, 1688–1850', *Economic History Review*, XXXIX (1986).
(4) **P. J. Cain** and **A. G. Hopkins,** 'Gentlemanly Capitalism and British Expansion Overseas, II. 'New Imperialism, 1850–1945', *Economic History Review*, XL (1987).
(5) **E. Davis** and **R. A. Huttenback,** with the assistance of Susan Grey Davis, *Mammon and the Pursuit of Empire: The Political Economy of British Imperialism, 1860–1912* (Cambridge, 1987).
(6) **A. G. Hopkins,** 'The Victorians and Africa: A Reconsideration of the Occupation of Egypt, 1882', *Journal of African History*, 27 (1986).
(7) **A. G. Hopkins,** 'Accounting for the British Empire', *Journal of Imperial and Commonwealth History*, 16 (1988).
(8) **W. R. Louis** (ed.), *Imperialism: The Robinson and Gallagher Controversy* (New York, 1976).
(9) **R. Robinson** and **J. Gallagher with A. Denny,** *Africa and the Victorians* (London, 2nd edn, 1981).
(10) **R. Owen** and **B. Sutcliffe** (eds), *Studies in the Theory of Imperialism* (London, 1972).

7 The Rise and Fall of the Managed Economy

R. MIDDLETON

'The common sense conclusion is that Britain and the other Western countries had full employment for a quarter of a century after the war because their governments were committed to full employment, and knew how to secure it; and they knew how to secure it because Keynes had told them how' (Michael Stewart). Yet, by 1979, it was said that 'anti-Keynesianism was the world's fastest growing industry'. How did this dramatic change come about, and what was the real contribution of the Keynesian revolution to economic policy and performance in Britain?

In the early post-war decades the view that governments knew how to control the economy and secure full employment was shared by both Labour and Conservative administrations. The policies which they adopted in pursuit of this aim were known as 'demand management' (see the box). But by the 1970s these policies were being repudiated by leading members of both parties. Recent research into the history of the managed economy in Britain has thrown new light on both the origins of the Keynesian revolution in economic policymaking and its eventual eclipse. A re-evaluation of the policies of the inter-war period, and of Keynes's theoretical contribution to post-war economic management, has been stimulated by the deterioration of Britain's economic performance since the early 1970s, and by the massive rise of unemployment since 1979. Just as the mass unemployment of the twenties and thirties gave credence to Keynesian ideas, so the economic troubles of the seventies and eighties strengthened support for his critics.

Demand Management: The central feature of the managed economy was the belief that the government could and should influence the economy-wide level of output and employment by changing the level of demand. This might be demand from households for consumer goods such as cars and TVs; or demand from firms for machinery and other capital goods; or the government's own demand, for school buildings, military equipment, and so forth. The principal instrument which the government could use to influence demand in the private sector was the level of taxation (fiscal policy). Thus taxes would be lowered in a recession, when it was desirable to stimulate demand; and raised in a boom, when it was thought necessary to restrict demand. Other instruments included interest rates, control over bank lending and hire-purchase regulations.

Deficit Finance: This refers to government expenditure which is financed by loans because it cannot be covered from revenue raised through taxation. An important part of the Keynesian revolution was the suggestion that the government should resort to Deficit Finance to raise demand and so reduce unemployment in a depression.

ECONOMIC MANAGEMENT BEFORE 1939

Until recently the natural corollary to views such as those held by Stewart was that if only Keynesian ideas had been adopted earlier, the inter-war unemployment problem could have been resolved. According to this view it was not until the theoretical wisdom of Keynes's *General Theory* (which was published in 1936), had been assimilated during the Second World War, that progress could be made towards the permanent attainment of full employment by proper management of the economy. Those who held this view also believed that the major obstacle to the earlier acceptance of Keynesian policies was the influence of a rival theory on an unthinking, orthodox

Treasury. This was the so-called 'classical' economic theory of an earlier age. A crucial premise of this theory was that deficit-financed expenditures (see the box) could only be made at the expense of a comparable volume of private expenditures. As a result no additional employment would be generated.

Official attitudes in the inter-war years, as shown in the Treasury's internal papers, have recently been re-examined by economic historians. [See Glynn and Booth (2) and Middleton (3) for summaries of this research.] Two major points have emerged. First, it has been shown that in fact considerable progress had been made towards acceptance of some aspects of the policy of demand management by 1939, but that this owed more to rearmament and political forces, than to Keynes and the economists.

Secondly, the Treasury view on deficit-finance has been subject to particularly detailed scrutiny. We now have a much better understanding of the reasons for the Treasury's rejection of the Keynesian message before the war. As indicated above, Keynes and his post-war followers laid most stress on the role of economic theory in determining official policy. By contrast, recent writers have emphasised the prevailing political and administrative constraints as limits to the potential efficacy of the Keynesian solution. The Treasury did not, as Keynes suggested, simply *assume* full employment, which would then, of course, have made it impossible to explain unemployment in theory or do something about it in practice. Rather, it pointed to factors such as the openness of the British economy, and the financial market's grave mistrust of increased government intervention. Given these features of Britain's economic position the Treasury attached great importance to the adverse effects which deficit-finance would have on the confidence of bankers and businessmen. If this confidence was lost, it would: (a) make it difficult for government to borrow, except at high interest rates: and (b) deter industrialists from making additions to their own capital equipment. The Treasury argued that these two unfavourable consequences might be more than enough to offset any gains from the initial government spending.

91

The 1944 White Paper on Employment Policy, which committed government to the 'maintenance of a high and stable level of employment', has traditionally been seen as the formal recognition of the principles of the Keynesian revolution in Britain. However, more recent research has revealed that the pace of official acceptance of Keynesian ideas was much slower than previously thought. Even after the 1944 White Paper, the Treasury remained reluctant to support long-term deficit-finance. The reason for this was not theoretical but political: the fear that there would be an explosion of expenditure once the fiscal discipline of a balanced budget was relaxed. If it was conceded that some expenditure might be covered by borrowing, the ability of governments to resist ever-growing popular demands for more money for housing, education, health services and so on would be greatly weakened. The Treasury also continued to emphasise its pre-war concerns about industrial efficiency, and argued that a policy of *general* demand management was no cure for unemployment caused by structural problems in *specific* industries or regions.

Tomlinson [5] went so far as to argue that there never was a Keynesian revolution. By this he meant that fiscal policy never became subordinate to the needs of employment creation, but was merely used as an instrument to control inflation and the balance of payments. While this view has found little support, there has been wider acceptance of his more limited conclusion that the role of economic theory in the policy process has been overstated, and that of administrative and political factors understated. This debate about the *application* of Keynesian ideas continues. There is, however, general agreement that during the war years the essential *theoretical* message of the Keynesian revolution – that capitalist economies were not self-stabilising by virtue of some automatic market mechanism – had been firmly accepted. At this date few economists would have denied that if the economy fell into a depression, with low levels of production and high unemployment, some form of government intervention would be needed to stimulate demand and help the economy get back to full employment.

The assessment of post-war economic management and of Britain's economic performance must be made in the context of the four major objectives of the policy-makers. Until the advent of Thatcherism these were: full employment, price stability, a surplus on the current account of the balance of payments, and economic growth. The central problem for economic management since the war has been the incompatibility of these objectives. Initially, the most difficult problem was to reconcile the desire for rapid economic growth with the need for a balance of payments surplus. Later, the main problem faced by the policy-makers was how to achieve full employment without at the same time encouraging more rapid increases in wages and prices. Some progress was made, but the position gradually deteriorated to the point where Britain seemed condemned to suffer both high unemployment and rapid inflation, while growth remained slow and the balance of payments weak.

This process can be seen in Figure 3. In the top chart the solid line shows unemployment as a percentage of the labour force, and the broken line shows the annual rate of increase of prices. The rise in both lines from the end of the 1960s is very striking. The bottom chart indicates Britain's inability to escape a recurrent deficit on the balance of payments. (The surplus (+) or deficit (−) on the balance of payments is kept in scale with the growth of the economy by expressing it as a percentage of gross domestic product − GDP.) These problems of unsuccessful economic management became the basis for increasingly severe crises, political as well as economic. By the 1970s this process culminated in the final rejection of the earlier consensus on the advantages of a Keynesian policy of economic management. We shall look briefly at each of these dilemmas to see how this came about.

In the early post-war decades the rate of economic growth in Britain was slow compared to that being achieved in countries like France, Germany, Italy and Japan, and there was considerable public pressure for more rapid expansion. The problem for economic management was that whenever growth speeded up, and unemployment dropped to very low

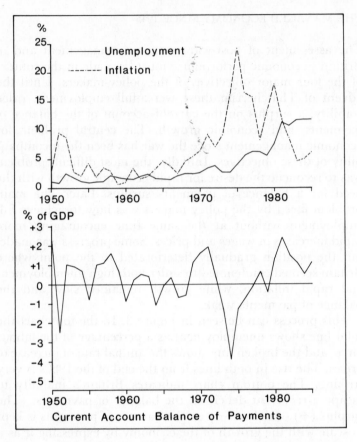

Figure 3 Inflation, unemployment and the balance of payments, 1950–85

levels, the balance of payments would get worse. This happened for several reasons: first, imports increased with the need for additional raw materials for industry; and exports fell as manufacturers preferred the easier option of selling in a booming home market. Secondly, as the economy moved closer to full capacity, there were shortages of both labour and materials. This stimulated higher wages and prices and this in turn harmed exports and helped imports. The result was a serious balance of payments crisis.

The government was forced to respond to this, and did so

94

by raising taxes, cutting government expenditure and generally acting to reduce demand in order to slow down the growth of the economy. This was the 'stop' phase of what came to be known as the 'stop-go' policy of demand management. Once economic activity had fallen to a lower level, and the balance of payments had improved, the political pressure for faster growth and lower unemployment would again be felt, and the weapons of economic management would be used to reverse the process, cutting taxes to stimulate demand: the 'go' phase. These cycles occurred repeatedly through the 1950s and 1960s, and are very evident in Figure 3.

The second dilemma which gradually emerged to cause acute problems for supporters of demand management was the trade-off between full employment and price stability. Initially the record was very good: from the end of the war until 1966, the proportion of the labour force unemployed was never greater than 2.5 per cent, and the rate of increase of wages and prices was reasonably satisfactory (see Figure 3). There was perhaps a tendency for prices to rise more rapidly than policy-makers would have wished, but it was not seen as a major problem. From the mid-1960s this situation changed dramatically. The precise reasons for this are still a matter of debate. Those who think the trouble started on the side of costs can point, in particular, to growing awareness on the part of organised workers of their ability to take advantage of full employment to press for higher wages. This ability had initially been restrained by fears of a return to the era of mass unemployment, but these fears were eroded as memories of the inter-war years faded, and a new and more militant generation entered the labour force. After 1969 this pressure on labour costs was strongly reinforced by the actions of the OPEC oil cartel.

On the other side of the debate are those who think costs can only have an impact on prices if the supply of money is increased to allow prices to rise. According to this view, it was the failure of the governments, both in Europe and the United States, to control the growth of the money supply which was responsible for the acceleration of inflation in the mid-sixties. Whatever the causes, the results of the process were very clear, and through the 1970s Britain was made increasingly aware of the new evil of 'stagflation', a previously unknown combination of slow growth and high unemployment with rapid inflation.

BRITAIN'S POST-WAR ECONOMIC PERFORMANCE

It is important to see Britain's post-war growth record in its historical perspective. The post-war record was good by the standards achieved by Britain in earlier periods. For example, the total quantity of goods and services produced each year (real GDP) grew at an average annual rate of 2.8 per cent over the years 1951–73, as compared with 2.2 per cent in the inter-war period 1924–37, and only 1.8 per cent over the pre-First World War period, 1873–1913. However, this improvement over historical standards was the common experience of our industrial competitors, and their post-war rate of growth was much better than ours: over the period 1950–73, the average for the six original members of the European Economic Community was over 5 per cent p.a., almost double the British rate. We thus need to understand both how we improved our own performance, and also why we did not do as well as others.

It is natural to ask about the relationship between Britain's relative success – by its own standards – in the post-war period, and the policies of economic managment. Was the Keynesian revolution in economic policy responsible for the post-war improvement in growth rates and, in particular, for the achievement of full employment? In a seminal paper of 1968, written before the long boom of the western economies had faltered, Matthews [reproduced in (1)] argued that Keynes's contribution was in fact only indirect, and that full employment could not have been the consequence of deficit financing because the budget was in surplus, not deficit, throughout this period. He attributed it instead to two other major features of the post-war period. The first was the high level of capital expenditure in industry, power supplies, transport, etc. This was undertaken to take advantage of the favourable investment opportunities created by the rapid technological advance in these years, and also to make good the backlog of investment needs which had been created during wartime and the prolonged depression of the inter-war years. The second stimulus for activity and employment was the boom in the world economy associated both with the rapid growth already noted in the EEC, Japan and other countries, and with the free trade policies which were generally introduced after the Second World War. This enabled Britain's exports to expand much more rapidly than had been possible in the depressed and tariff-protected markets of the inter-war years.

Although Matthews was criticised for the way in which he measured the government's surplus, the essence of his argument survived. It was sufficient for Tomlinson [5] to make the important observation that the highly fortunate set of circumstances of the 1950s and 1960s led to an exaggeration of the government's capacity to deliver a high level of activity and full employment in adverse conditions. This misunderstanding of the power of Keynesian policies was in turn a contributory factor in the subsequent disillusionment with demand management. Too much was expected of these policies, and their inability to live up to these expectations made them more vulnerable when faced by the combined challenge posed by monetarist economics and changes in political attitudes.

THE CRISIS OF DEMAND MANAGEMENT

In 1979 the consensus in support of the post-war Keynesian revolution was broken. Thatcher's newly-elected Conservative government formally abandoned the macroeconomic objectives that had been adhered to (though not necessarily achieved) by all former governments. The new administration explicitly denied that stabilisation by means of demand management was either possible or desirable; and it asserted its belief in an older tradition of a liberal market order with a minimum of state intervention. It was the impossibility of reconciling full employment with price stability which was

97

most immediately responsible for undermining the Keynesian era, since wage stability had always depended in part upon the possibility of unemployment. For a time, it was thought that all that was required to sustain a programme of demand management was a refinement of its techniques, and the addition of more effective incomes policies to regulate the growth of wages. Gradually, however, it was recognised that some more fundamental adjustment was called for.

The other major forces which contributed to the political success of the counter-revolution included:
* new developments in economic theory associated with monetarist ideas;
* increased political hostility to the power of government, involving not only demand management but also matters like the level of taxation and the extent of public ownership;
* a new analysis of what was responsible for the long-run decline in Britain's relative economic position, with an emphasis on political and cultural factors; and
* the deterioration in the international economic environment, and the breakdown of some of the key post-war agreements on exchange rates and trade.

MONETARISM

We begin with monetarism. For policy purposes this doctrine had two important elements: the quantity theory of money and the natural rate of unemployment. According to the former, the supply of money can only change as a result of actions by the monetary authorities; and as the money supply changes (with other relevant factors remaining broadly constant), the price level will change proportionately. The cause of inflation is thus the government's action in increasing the money supply.

The natural rate of unemployment hypothesis holds that the economy has a tendency to return to a certain rate of unemployment (determined by institutional factors such as the bargaining strength of trade unions). Any policy which tries to move unemployment away from this natural rate may succeed in the short term, but only at the expense of accelerating inflation in the long term. From this it follows that instead of pursuing full employment goals macroeconomic policy ought to be limited solely to the pursuit of a constant rate of growth of money supply. This, in turn, would stabilise the growth of money incomes.

Thus, monetarists rule out the possibility that demand management can affect either real output (as opposed to its money value, which can increase as prices rise), or employment, *in the long run*. In sharp contrast to the Keynesian view that market economies were not self-stabilising, the monetarists revived the argument that they were. For them, it was precisely this self-stabilising property of the economy which invalidated the whole of post-war (Keynesian) demand management. They argued that such policies did not, and could not, create employment, but only inflation. In this way demand management seriously damaged the free market economy, for which *price stability* is an essential foundation.

SUPPLY-SIDE POLICIES

A second feature of the monetarist approach to economic policy was the emphasis on what came to be known as 'supply-side policies'. For the reasons just given it rejected any role for demand management policies. However, it accepted that governments could take action to improve economic performance by microeconomic policies aimed at influencing *individual* households or firms or industries from the supply side.

One aspect of this approach which was given immediate attention was the policy of lowering marginal tax rates for those with high incomes. This was intended to increase incentives, and generate increased managerial and entrepreneurial contributions to economic progress. For those on low incomes, the corresponding incentives were to be achieved by a reduction of unemployment benefits (particularly the earnings-related payments) relative to wages. Other areas of policy approached from this supply-side perspective included various attempts to increase competition and to reduce monopoly powers exercised by certain groups. This was directed particularly at the trade unions. It was believed that by reducing trade union power it would be possible to achieve both lower inflation and more favourable conditions for the modernisation of British industry.

This view was bolstered by a major study by a distinguished American scholar, Mancur Olson [4]. He argued that slow growth could be attributed to the development of 'distributional coalitions': interest groups such as medieval guilds, trade unions or employers' associations. By seeking to gain or maintain advantages for their members, these groups slowed down a society's capacity to adopt new technologies and to reallocate resources in response to changing conditions. The longer such groups were allowed to operate undisturbed, the greater would be their power and thus their ability to retard growth. His argument was illustrated by a wide range of cases from different historical periods and countries; but the long period of political and social stability which Britain has enjoyed, without the shock of revolution or military defeat, gives his analysis a particular relevance to the British case.

CONCLUSIONS

One valuable consequence of the recent work on the Keynesian revolution by economic historians is that we now have a much clearer appreciation of policy constraints facing governments in their conduct of macroeconomic policies. The traditional preoccupation of economic historians with the long term can also be used to good effect, given that the roots of the 'British disease' clearly pre-date Keynes, let alone his legacy of demand management. The task now is to use this information and understanding, and to work with other disciplines to produce a broader and better analysis of Britain's economic problems.

REFERENCES AND FURTHER READING

(1) **C. H. Feinstein** (ed.), *The Managed Economy: Essays in British Economic Policy and Performance since 1929* (Oxford, 1983).
(2) **S. Glynn and A. Booth** (eds), *The Road to Full Employment* (London, 1987).
(3) **R. Middleton,** *Towards the Managed Economy: Keynes, the Treasury, and the Fiscal Policy Debate of the 1930s* (London, 1985).
(4) **M. Olson,** *The Rise and Decline of Nations: Economic Growth, Stagflation and Social Rigidities* (New Haven, 1982).
(5) **J. Tomlinson,** *British Macroeconomic Policy since 1940* (London, 1985).
(6) **A. Gamble,** *Britain in Decline: Economic policy, political strategy and the British state* (London, second edn, 1985).

III Society

8 Population Growth: England, 1680–1820

E. A. WRIGLEY

Though it has long been agreed that population growth accelerated sharply in the course of the 'long' eighteenth century (1680–1820), there have been sharp differences of view about the reason for the acceleration. The disagreements have extended both to what might be termed demographic mechanics (i.e. the relative parts played by changes in birth and death rates), and to the wider context of the change. In what follows I shall describe the results of recent research which appears to have settled the controversy regarding the immediate demographic mechanics of the remarkable spurt in growth rates. Wider issues, such as the interplay between economic circumstances and the tempo of birth, marriage and death, also merit discussion in the light of the new findings, and are touched on briefly at the end of this essay.

THE OLD ARGUMENT

If a population is to pass from a stationary state to one of rapid growth, it is evident either that mortality must fall considerably, or fertility must rise substantially, or there must be some combination of the two of a less extreme kind. It might have been expected that differences of interpretation concerning the relative importance of the two factors would have narrowed as the volume of research increased. This has not proved to be the case. In recent years it has been argued at one extreme that the bulk of the acceleration was due to increased fertility [Krause (3)]; and at the other that the sole reason for increasingly rapid population growth lay in falling mortality [McKeown (4)]. There have also been, of course, many more shaded views; notable amongst them the judicious writings of Habakkuk (2). In general the 'pro-mortality' arguments have held the field. McKeown's confident and lucid exposition of the argument that it was unnecessary to look beyond a fall in mortality for an explanation has been particularly influential.

The lack of progress in resolving an old argument has a simple explanation. In the 1970s no less than in the 1800s the prime source of empirical information about population movements in the eighteenth century lay in the parish register abstracts collected by John Rickman. The first census was taken in 1801 in the wake of a lively debate about the growth of population in the preceding century. As a response to this debate, Rickman – who supervised the census operations – not only collected information about those living in 1801 but also approached the incumbent of every parish asking for tabulations of the totals of baptisms, burials and marriages registered at intervals over the course of the century since 1700. Unfortunately, the abstracts suffer from defects so serious that Flinn remarked of results based on them that 'whether in the form of totals of population or of the vital rates' they 'are built on such shifting sand as to make them virtually unacceptable for the purposes of modern scholarship'. It was known from the first that the number of births and deaths greatly exceeded the number of recorded baptisms and burials. But it proved difficult to establish the extent of the shortfall in either case, and equally difficult to determine the timing and extent of the deterioration in registration as the century progressed. Furthermore Rickman had collected the baptism and burial data only for every tenth year prior to 1780; only for marriages had he requested annual totals from 1754 onwards.

Nor did the problems end with deficiencies in the data. Even if registration had been complete, there would still have been major uncertainties in the absence of more sophisticated techniques of analysis. Once again the fundamental difficulty was straightforward. Conventional demographic measures

106

Table 8   The growth of population in England (less Monmouth)
during the 'long' eighteenth century

	Total population (000s)	Compound annual percentage growth rate over preceding decade
1681	4930	
1691	4931	0.0
1701	5058	0.3
1711	5230	0.3
1721	5350	0.2
1731	5263	−0.2
1741	5576	0.6
1751	5772	0.3
1761	6147	0.6
1771	6448	0.5
1781	7042	0.9
1791	7740	0.9
1801	8664	1.1
1811	9886	1.3
1821	11492	1.5

Source: Wrigley and Schofield, *Population History of England*,
table A3.1, pp. 528–9.

depend upon enumerating a population at risk (the *stock*,
usually obtained from a census); counting the number of
events of a particular type (the *flow*, usually taken from vital
registration); and then deriving a *rate* to express the incidence
of the phenomenon. Thus, calculating a crude birth rate
implies knowledge of the total population and of the total flow
of births. Again, age-specific mortality rates usually depend
on, say, knowing the total of men aged 25–29 and the number
of deaths in that age group. But before 1801 there were no
censuses, and so without a stock it was hard to employ
conventional methods successfully. It seemed doubtful
whether even the simplest types of rates could be cajoled out
of the kind of evidence available; and if crude birth and death
rates could not be estimated with confidence, *a fortiori* more
refined measures could not be derived.

Both the data deficiencies and the technical problems, however, have been largely overcome in recent years and as a result some old conundrums now appear much less baffling. The technical problems have been solved by two developments. The first, *family reconstitution*, depends upon being able to link together records relating to the individuals comprising a family. It is feasible only where register entries name those whose baptisms, marriages and burials are recorded, and provide sufficient information to identify each individual unambiguously. Though laborious, family reconstitution can provide very detailed and accurate information about the demographic history of individual parishes. The second, *back projection*, in contrast needs only totals of events. But provided they can be 'anchored' to a census with reliable age data at the end of the data series, the technique will yield estimates of population totals at any desired intervals, as well as details of age structure, crude birth, death and marriage rates and estimates of net migration. It also provides the information needed to calculate two of the most useful general demographic measures: the gross reproduction rate and expectation of life at birth. [Wrigley (5) and Wrigley and Schofield (7).] These measures are defined in the box.

The data problems have been tackled by returning to the source which Rickman tapped. The best quality registers have been used for reconstitution work; and monthly totals of baptisms, burials and marriages have been counted for a sample of 400 parish registers over the whole period from the establishment of the parish register sytem in 1538 to the inception of state vital registration in 1837. Suitably corrected for the several sources of bias, error and deficiency in registration, they can be made to yield estimates of the national totals of births, deaths and marriages from the last years of Henry VIII until the start of Victoria's reign.

Combining new methods with new data the course of change in the 'long' eighteenth century is at last laid bare. Table 8 shows the growth in population occurring in England between 1681 and 1821, and the compound annual growth rates prevailing in each decade. The total population rose by

Gross reproduction rate (GRR) measures the number of girl babies which would be born to the average woman at prevailing fertility rates assuming she survived to the end of the child-bearing period. It is therefore a 'pure' measure of fertility.

Expectation of life at birth (e_0) is similarly a 'pure' measure of mortality. It expresses the number of years a new-born child will live at prevailing age-specific mortality rates. It is, therefore, unaffected by adventitious factors such as the current age structure of the population.

133 per cent between the two dates, but growth was heavily concentrated in the second half of the 140-year period. There are no surprises, though the slightness of growth in the first 50 years should be emphasised: in 1731 the population was only 7 per cent larger than in 1681, equivalent to a crude birth rate only 1.3 per thousand per annum higher than the crude death rate over the period in question.

FERTILITY V. MORTALITY

Figure 4 conveys a first impression of the background to the great changes of the period by plotting the paths of the crude birth and death rates. The rates relate to 5-year periods centring on the dates shown. This dampens considerably the more hectic movement of the annual rates and makes it easier to identify longer-term trends. Until about 1710 any gap between the two rates was minor, but thereafter they drew further and further apart until by the early nineteenth century the birth rate was about 50 per cent higher than the death rate. The general impression conveyed by the behaviour of the two lines is that rising fertility contributed more than falling mortality to the surge in the growth rate. Crude rates, however, are sometimes a fallible guide to the underlying situation making it desirable to consider more refined measures; in particular the gross reproduction rates and the expectation of life at birth defined above.

109

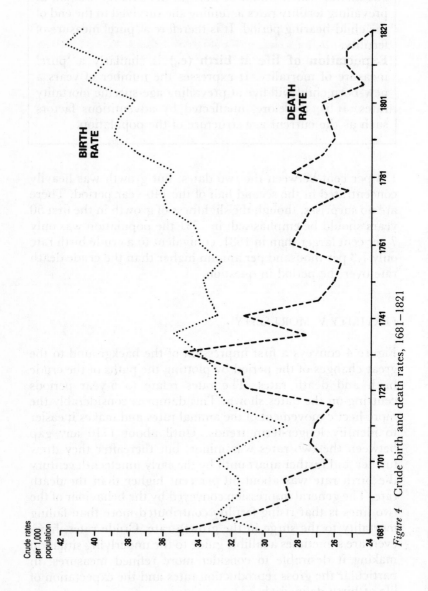

Figure 4 Crude birth and death rates, 1681–1821

These two measures are plotted in Figure 5. This shows that the GRR rose by almost 50 per cent from slightly over 2.0 to almost 3.0 in the course of the 'long' eighteenth century, while expectation of life (e_0) rose by little more than 20 per cent from about 32 to 39 years. It should be noted that, in order still further to lessen the impact of short-term influences, the plotted values refer to 15-year periods centring on the years shown.

Although the GRR and e_0 are less familiar measures than the crude birth and death rate, they have valuable analytic properties which serve to determine the question over which so much ink has been spilt since Rickman's day.

Using the data shown in Figure 5 it can be demonstrated that two-thirds or more of the acceleration in population growth during the 'long' eighteenth century was due to the rise in fertility and only one-third or less to improved mortal-

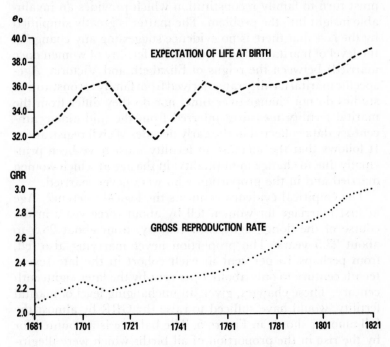

Figure 5 Expectation of life at birth and the gross reproduction rate, 1681–1821

ity. It can also be shown that for mortality alone to have accounted for the whole of the acceleration, it would have had to have improved by as great a margin proportionately between 1680 and 1820 as it was to do during the great period of medical advance between 1820 and the end of the Second World War. This consideration underscores the implausibility of the more extreme positions adopted at times by the advocates of mortality change as the exclusive key to population growth before the nineteenth century.

REASONS FOR THE RISE IN FERTILITY

What then caused the very substantial fertility rise which occurred? The data presented so far are all derived from the technique of back projection. To solve this further issue we must turn to family reconstitution which provides an invaluable insight into the problem. The matter is greatly simplified by the fact that there is no evidence suggesting any change in the level of marital fertility (that is the fertility of women once married) between the reigns of Elizabeth and Victoria. Age-specific marital fertility rates derived from family reconstitution studies do not change over time, nor do they differ from the marital fertility measures inferred from the mid-nineteenth-century data collected in the early decades of civil registration. It follows that the increase in fertility must have been principally due to change in nuptiality: in the age at which women married and in the proportion who were never married.

The empirical evidence confirms the logical inference. Age at first marriage for women fell by about three years in the course of the 'long' eighteenth century: from about 26.5 to about 23.5 years. The proportion never marrying also fell, from perhaps 15 per cent in each cohort in the late seventeenth century to only about 7 per cent by the later eighteenth century. These changes, given an unchanging level of marital fertility, would have sufficed to raise the GRR by almost the full amount shown in Figure 5. The balance is accounted for by the rise in the proportion of all births which were illegitimate, but this made only a small contribution to the overall rise in fertility. Changes in marriage patterns, in short, prove

112

to have been the main reason for the move from a stationary population to a peak rate of growth.

Space does not permit more than a cursory survey of the implications of the knowledge recently gained, but two further comments may serve to suggest the considerations that are likely to figure prominently as research takes new directions.

MARRIAGE, LIVING STANDARDS AND ECONOMIC GROWTH

First, the discovery that marriage was the key variable whose fluctuations largely governed growth trends suggests that attention should be devoted to those social and economic circumstances that influenced marriage decisions. In all societies, marriage is a highly deliberate act attracting the earnest attention not simply of the principals to the marrage, but also of their parents, of a wider network of kin, and of society *en large*. In western Europe, however, apparently uniquely, its timing was not effectively determined by a biological trigger. Elsewhere, marriage for women was closely associated with the attainment of sexual maturity. Shame and disgrace attached to any girl and to her immediate kin if she were to fail to find a husband at this period of life. In consequence marriage was very early and virtually universal, so that only 1 or 2 in 100 women never married, usually because of conspicuous mental or physical handicap. In western Europe, in contrast, marriage close to menarche was very rare and women spent an average of about 10 years sexually adult but unmarried. Moreover, many never married. Characteristically, the average female age at first marriage lay in the range 23 to 27 years and between 5 and 20 per cent never married.

In England there is evidence that marriage was sensitive, both in the short term and in the long, to economic circumstances. Not only were years of high prices years when fewer couples came to the church porch, but a secular improvement or deterioration in real incomes was mirrored by rises or falls in nuptiality. Such trends often covered many successive decades. In consequence there was greater scope for a successful adjustment between numbers and available resources than

113

in other pre-industrial societies. There is also evidence to suggest that the relatively high standard of living achieved in early modern England may be partly a result of the way in which the 'European' marriage system functioned in an English setting. It is an element which should probably figure in any discussion of the background to the industrial revolution. The general point is straightforward: if marriage behaviour was sensitive to economic circumstances, severe pressure of population on resources could be avoided, people could enjoy relatively high real incomes, and there could be a greater opportunity for economic changes of a type likely to foster growth. But the 'European' marriage system also conferred a number of specific advantages. For example, since the age structure of a population is very largely determined by its fertility, the late marriage and associated low fertility found in England resulted in a favourable dependency ratio, with proportionately many fewer children to support than in countries like India or China. Again, the fact that women spent many of their most vigorous years in the labour force without the distraction of marriage and dependent children probably produced patterns of earnings, savings and expenditure unlike those in societies with a different marriage system.

DYNAMICS OF A 'LOW-PRESSURE' DEMOGRAPHY

Second, there is a related topic representing an intriguing paradox about the population history of England over the whole early modern period. Her population almost quadrupled between 1550 and 1820 (from 3.0 to 11.5 millions), while the populations of other European countries grew much more modestly. France, Germany, Italy and Spain all grew by between 50 and 80 per cent [Wrigley (6)]. The contrast is striking. It began a process which by 1900 had resulted in England joining France, Italy and Germany as the 'big four' of western Europe with roughly similar populations, whereas in contrast in the mid-sixteenth century the populations of the other three were between four and six times the English total. Yet England had a 'low-pressure' demography with both fertility and mortality at modest levels compared with all extra-European areas, and even compared with many other parts of western Europe.

It is easy to show that, on plausible assumptions about pre-industrial economies, a 'low-pressure' demography in societies where it is difficult to secure a rapid growth in total output will result (other things being equal) in a higher equilibrium level of real incomes than in the 'high-pressure' case with both birth and death rates at a high level. People are less numerous but more prosperous. English history, however, suggests that the *dynamics* of population and economy under 'low-pressure' conditions may be such that a more rapid growth in both output and population is attainable than would be possible where 'high pressure' prevailed. Relatively high real incomes may bring benefits through their impact on the structure of demand, savings and capital investment that facilitate economic growth, allowing numbers to rise without simultaneously depressing living standards. The same characteristics which imply a low population *at a given point in time* may permit relatively rapid growth *over time*.

In a brief compass, simplifications which entail a failure to do justice to the complexity of historical change are hard to avoid. Both in sketching the course and manner of population growth in eighteenth-century England in the light of new knowledge, and in outlining the implications of the new situation, this problem has no doubt been exemplified. The price of brevity is partial distortion. If there is a countervailing benefit, it may lie in the ease with which salient points can be picked out. English population history has shed some long-standing uncertainties and acquired striking new attributes in recent years. It serves a useful purpose to recount them rather starkly so that what is novel is more readily distinguished.

REFERENCES AND FURTHER READING

(1) **M. W. Flinn,** *British Population Growth 1700–1850* (London, 1970).
(2) **H. J. Habakkuk,** 'English population in the eighteenth century', in D. V. Glass and D. E. C. Eversley (eds), *Population in History* (London, 1965).

(3) **J. T. Krause,** 'Changes in English fertility and mortality, 1780–1850', *Economic History Review*, 2nd series, XI (1958).
(4) **T. McKeown,** *The Modern Rise of Population* (London, 1976).
(5) **E. A. Wrigley** (ed.), *An Introduction to English Historical Demography* (London, 1966).
(6) **E. A. Wrigley,** 'The growth of population in eighteenth-century England: a conundrum resolved', *Past and Present*, 98 (1983).
(7) **E. A. Wrigley** and **R. S. Schofield,** *The Population History of England 1541–1871. A Reconstruction* (London, 1981).

9 Standards of Living and Industrialisation

R. FLOUD

Generations of students of modern British economic and social history have wrestled with 'the standard of living debate'. Not for nothing has Peter Mathias [4] called it the 'most sustained single controversy in British economic history'. Under the guise of the 'condition of England question' it obsessed men of the mid-nineteenth century as diverse as Engels, Disraeli, Chadwick and Macaulay, while in the twentieth century it has been central to the work of such distinguished historians as Ashton, Clapham, Hartwell, Hobsbawm and Thompson. Many different intellectual approaches have been used in the debate; this essay considers a new way of describing changes in the standard of living by measuring the height of the British population in the past.

MEASURING LIVING STANDARDS

The issues have been formulated and reformulated in many ways but the core question remains: what was the impact of the industrial revolution in Britain upon the standard of living of the British working class? Even such an apparently clear question conceals many problems: what do we mean by 'impact'; when was 'the Industrial Revolution'; how do we define the 'working class'; how do we measure changes in the 'standard of living'?

Measurement is central to the standard of living debate, as to so many other issues in history. If we cannot agree on how to measure change, we can neither describe nor analyse it. In

117

this instance, the central issue is about how to measure the 'standard of living'. For much of the twentieth century, the standard of living has been defined as the average money income of the workers divided by the price of the 'basket of goods' which those workers bought. This calculation has been performed in two ways, which can best be described as the 'bottom-up' and 'top-down' approaches.

The bottom-up approach relies on the collection of numerous examples of the wages which were paid to groups of workers; these wages are then averaged to give a *per capita* money wage. The top-down approach, by contrast, begins by estimating the overall value of the payments made for the goods and services produced by the economy during a year, the national income, which is then divided by the size of the population to give an estimate of national income *per capita*. Both annual series of *per capita* estimates are normally expressed as index numbers. The series are then compared with information about prices. The bottom-up approach uses the price of a basket of goods representing the purchases of a representative consumer from among the working class. The top-down approach uses as many as possible of the prices of all goods and services which have been produced. Dividing wages by prices then gives indices of real wages or real income.

In practice, both methods are much more complicated, so that using and reconciling them has given rise to much debate. The technicalities divert attention from the more fundamental question: what do measures of real income or real wages actually tell us about the standard of living? The answer is that, properly measured, they tell us a great deal. Knowledge of the income and spending habits of our neighbour today tells us much about his or her occupation, life-style and attitudes, just as knowledge of the real wages of a man or woman in the past illuminates their lives. And just as today we learn a great deal about different countries by comparing their national incomes *per capita*, so we can learn from a comparison of national income of one country over a long period of time.

Neither real wages nor real income tell us everything about the way in which people lived in the past. As Eric Hobsbawm [3] once put it in a discussion of this topic: 'Man does not live by bread alone'; there is much more to life than one's inflation-adjusted wage at one moment in time.

An obvious omission is the length of one's life. The expectation of life at birth in England and Wales rose from about 35 years in 1780 to about 40 years in 1840, most of the rise occurring before 1820. In other words, on average each person lived five years longer, although there continued to be wide variations in length of life between different social groups and between people living in different parts of the country. To put it in yet another way, as a whole people enjoyed their real income or real wage for 14 per cent longer if they lived in 1840 than if they lived in 1780. To most of us, this would represent a considerable improvement in our standard of living, yet it is one that is entirely ignored by the normal measures of growth in real income or real wages; these measures compare the income or wage at one point in time, not lifetime earnings.

Other examples can be given; some are seen as improvements in the standard of living like access to new imported foods, but many, such as the spread of waterborne infections in the crowded cities, would normally be thought to have depressed living standards. The smoke pollution of nineteenth-century cities is an example which faces both ways; it demonstrates the growth of factories which gave wider access to employment and pay to provide homes with coal fires while, at the same time, it condemned many city dwellers to death from respiratory disease.

It is possible, therefore, to catalogue many aspects of life which are not summed up in measures of real income or wages. If all of them changed over time in the same way as real income or wages, then there would be little problem; but as the example of smoke pollution shows, they did not. How then can we sum them up and allow these aspects of life to contribute to our picture of living standards in the past?

One way is to begin with a measure of real income or wages and to adjust it up or down in relation to other aspects of

119

living standards. If life expectation increased by 10 per cent over a particular period, on top of a 15 per cent increase in wages, we could conclude that living standards rose by 25 per cent. But there are problems. It is not easy, for example, to assess the proportion by which pollution increased, particularly as it varied so much from town to country, nor to assess the benefit of improved access to new consumer goods like cotton cloth.

In addition, it is also very likely that we will count the same thing twice. This can happen in two ways: first, it is not fanciful to think that some of the 15 per cent increase in wages was used to buy some of the 10 per cent increase in life expectation, through better food or an improved water supply. Second, two changes may run in parallel; it is very difficult to separate out improvements in the chances of catching a particular disease from improvements in the chances of surviving that disease. Both increase living standards, but they are not easily pulled apart.

Despite the immense amount that we have learned about changes in real income and real wages and other aspects of living standards, it therefore still makes sense to continue the search for other ways of measurement and to explore how those other ways add to our knowledge of the past. In such a search it makes sense also to explore how investigators describe changes in living standards which are occurring around us today.

THE CONCEPT OF NUTRITIONAL STATUS

One such method is that of the measurement of nutritional status. Historians have long been interested in changes in diet and in the nutrition which we receive and have received in the past. But human biologists have increasingly emphasised that nutrition or diet is only part of the story. Our bodies take in food and warmth and use such nutrients to maintain them in working order and, in childhood and adolescence, to grow; we also need nutrients to sustain work effort and to combat disease. If we do not get enough nutrients in relation to these tasks, we will be unable to perform all of them effectively; this may lead us to be less active or work less hard, but this is likely soon to reduce our incomes. The downward spiral into malnutrition is a common feature of the less developed world.

Human biologists use the term 'nutritional status' to describe the state of the human body as it balances nutrient intake with growth, work and the defeat of disease. They have found that, although various indicators are available, probably the best indicator of that balance is height and the speed of growth of height during childhood and adolescence. This is so both in individuals and in groups, although in slightly different ways.

We all follow the same pattern of growth, shown in Figure 6. This shows distribution of heights by percentiles. Thus the 97th centile indicates that 97 per cent of the males are below the height shown for each age, and only 3 per cent above that. Similarly, the 50th centile (more usually known as the median), divides the males so that half are taller than the height shown and half are shorter. And the 3rd centile indicates that 97 per cent of the males are above, and only 3 per cent below, the height shown for each age. Our place on the chart reflects a mixture of genetic inheritance from our parents, some random factors and the effects of the environment in which we are brought up. If that environment alters, for example because we suffer serious disease, starvation or even psychological trauma, our growth falters and may even stop, forcing us from one of the lines shown in Figure 6 to another. This has been observed in many recent cases of child abuse.

When we consider not individuals but the height of an entire group of people, then genetic, random and environmental factors produce together in one age-group a range of heights. But because the genetic and random components change extremely slowly, almost all change over time in the average height of a group of people can be attributed to the effects of the changing environment. In other words, changes in average height (measuring changes in nutritional status) sum up changing living conditions.

The impact of the environment on nutritional status, as measured by indicators such as average height, is very complex. In particular, the human body can respond to sustained periods of deprivation or disease by growing more slowly but for longer periods; groups of people in the under-

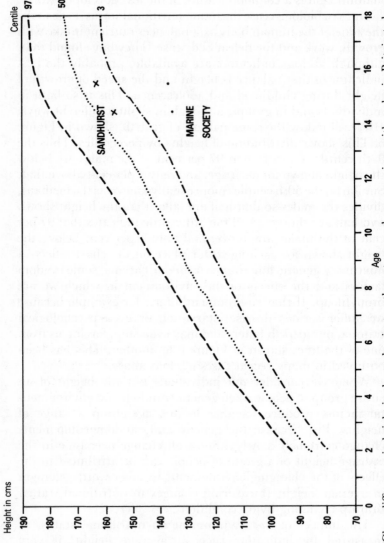

Figure 6 Class differences in height in the early nineteenth century, and a comparison with males in Britain today

developed world can appear very short by the standards of the developed world while they are children or teenagers but, by continuing to grow longer than is now the pattern in the developed world, can make up much of the deficit by the time they reach adulthood. This makes it important to examine the whole profile of growth, such as that in Figure 6, and to be careful always to use standards which are age-related.

HISTORIANS AND NUTRITIONAL STATUS: HOW CAN HISTORIANS USE THIS KNOWLEDGE?

*First, changes in the average height of a population or sub-group within a population can be used as an indicator of changes in nutritional status: it is common knowledge that the average height of people in many countries has changed markedly during this century and this implies that average nutritional status has improved.
*Second, differences in the average height of different groups provide a good indication of their relative nutritional status; even today, there are significant differences in the average height of different social classes in Britain, and these differences were greater in the past.
*Third, there is good evidence linking nutritional status with the impact of particular diseases; study of height helps us to explain the prevalence of those diseases in the past.

Let us take first social class. Table 9 shows the average height of men and women in different social classes today and a century ago; although the classification systems differ, it is clear that social differences were much greater then than today. These differences, although clear in adulthood, were much more marked during childhood and adolescence, for the reasons which were mentioned above. One particularly dramatic illustration of the size of class differences in the early nineteenth century can be drawn from two archives, those of the Marine Society of London and those of the Royal Military Academy at Sandhurst.

The Marine Society was founded in 1756 as a charity devoted to helping both poor children and the Royal and

Table 9   Socio-economic differences in average height in the
1880s and today (cm)

	Age 18 The 1880s		Age 16–19 The 1980s
Social Class:			
Professional	173.4	I and II	176.5
Commercial	171.3	III non-manual	174.8
Town Artisan	166.6	III manual	174.7
Labouring	169.0	IV and V	173.0

Sources: The 1880s: Final Report of the Anthropometric
Committee of the Association for the Advancement
of Science (London, 1883).
The 1980s: Adult Heights and Weights. The Report
of a Survey by the OPCS (London, 1984).

merchant navies by taking children from the streets of London
and finding them sea-going jobs. Between 1770 and 1870
about fifty thousand boys were helped in this way and the
Society kept records of all these boys and of their parents;
among the information collected was the age and height of
each boy. Starting from a slightly later date, in 1806, the
Royal Military Academy collected the same information, but
about a very different set of boys. Their recruits were the
children of the aristocracy, of the higher ranks of officers in the
army and navy and, to some extent, of the professional classes.
Figure 6 shows the contrast in the heights of these two
groups of boys at one age (14) and at one point in time,
although the records allow for many more such comparisons.
It can be calculated that the two distributions of heights
hardly overlap, so that nearly all upper-class boys were taller
at that age than nearly all boys from the lower working class.
Such extreme differences would certainly have diminished in
adulthood but would still have remained both large by
modern standards and immediately visible to a casual observer. Flinn [2] quotes one of the Factory Inspectors who
remarked after a visit to a particularly deprived group of
handloom weavers in 1840 that: 'They are decayed in their
bodies; the whole race of them is rapidly descending to the size

of Liliputians. You could not raise a grenadier company amongst them all.'

Figure 6 also shows how short both groups of boys were by modern standards. The contrast is greatest for the boys of the Marine Society: they were shorter by far than any group of children in the developed world today and shorter than most groups in the developing world, the nearest comparison being some peoples of the New Guinea highlands. Their height is incontrovertible evidence of the deprivation of the working classes in the early nineteenth century. But the Sandhurst boys, despite their privileged backgrounds, were not as tall as a similar group from the upper class would be today. Some possible reasons are discussed below.

LONG-TERM CHANGES

While the extent of deprivation among working-class children in the early nineteenth century is surprising, its existence is not. That deprivation is fully documented by contemporary observers and explained by the income levels which have been calculated. If the evidence of heights is to be useful to historians, that evidence must also tell us something about the long-term changes which have occurred in the height, and thus in the nutritional status, of groups within the British population.

Here we must confront the evidence. It was not until 1980 that a sample survey was taken of the heights of British adults, although information about children derived from school medical inspection dates back to just before the First World War. For earlier periods we must rely on data which were collected originally for other purposes; with some exceptions, such as the Marine Society, this means data from the armed forces. The records of millions of recruits, including their ages and heights, were collected from the middle of the eighteenth century onwards and are deposited in the Public Record Office.

These records have advantages and disadvantages. Their major advantage is that they describe millions of members of the working class and that the information can easily be classified by the civilian occupation and the places of birth and recruitment of the soldier, sailor or marine. Comparison with other evidence also shows that, although military recruitment was largely voluntary, it drew very widely from the working class; there is no evidence that military recruits were in actuality, as opposed to popular mythology, drawn largely from the dregs of the population.

The major disadvantage of this evidence stems, paradoxically, from the identification of height with nutritional status. Because military recruiters were convinced, from their own observation, that tall soldiers were better nourished and better able to stand up to the rigours of a military life, their first means of discrimination between potential recruits was on the basis of height. Different military units applied different standards, but all rejected some short men and the details of those men therefore do not normally appear in the military records. The records which do exist are thus a biased sample of working-class men, excluding the short, and any average height calculated from them will be biased.

The statistical methods which have been used to cope with this problem are complex in detail but simple in conception. A height distribution follows the bell-shaped curve of the normal distribution. The military records typically give us a distribution which follows such a curve from the top downwards until the point at which the recruiting officer rejected short men. But because the shape of the curve is so well defined, we can therefore use the upper part of the curve to estimate the shape of the full curve and, from this, can estimate the average height corrected for the sample bias.

Using these methods, we can then estimate the long-term changes which have occurred in the heights of British men since the middle of the eighteenth century, as in Figure 7. This shows that heights rose in the late eighteenth and early nineteenth centuries, reaching a peak among those born in the second and third decades of the century, before beginning a decline which was then only gradually reversed during the rest of the century. Much more rapid growth occurred in the twentieth century, as it did in every other country in the developed world. British heights have during that period been surpassed by those of a number of other northern European

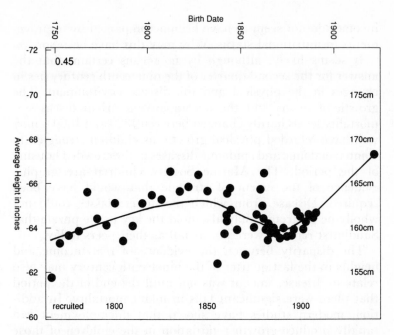

Figure 7 Average heights of males recruited to the army at the age of eighteen, 1750 onwards. (The dates of birth are given at the top and the date of their recruitment along the bottom.)

nations; the Dutch and Norwegians are now the tallest national populations in the world.

These results provide an important supplement to the evidence drawn from studies of incomes as a component in the debate on the standard of living. Although, as Crafts showed in Chapter 5, the results of those studies have been constantly revised, they show substantial growth in real incomes in the late eighteenth and early nineteenth centuries, a period when the height data suggest a substantial improvement in nutritional status and when mortality fell sharply. Similarly, the evidence for rising real incomes and improvements in health and in nutritional status in the twentieth century is unambiguous.

The important new contribution of the height data lies in the second quarter of the nineteenth century and during the so-called Great Depression towards the end of the century. In both periods, substantial improvements in real wages and

127

incomes do not seem to have been accompanied by improvements in nutritional status. Why may this have been so?

It seems likely, although by no means certain, that the answer for the second quarter of the nineteenth century lies in changes in the physical and the disease environment. The growth of towns and the accompanying urban diseases – mortality levels hardly changed between 1820 and 1860 – may well have retarded physical growth, as children struggled to combat endemic and epidemic diseases in the crowded housing of the period. The Marine Society children are graphic evidence of the extent of struggle that would have been required. Disease, from which the upper classes could not wholly be protected, may also hold the key to the puzzle that Sandhurst recruits were not as tall as their peers today.

The disparity between the evidence of real income and heights in the last quarter of the nineteenth century may also relate to disease, since it was not until the end of the period that there were significant falls in infant mortality. In addition, modern studies have shown that unemployment can rapidly produce growth retardation in the children of those affected. It may be that the evidence of heights is an indication of the severity of unemployment, which is known to be a feature of this period, but is very difficult to measure.

POSSIBILITIES FOR THE FUTURE

Height data offer many more possibilities. It has not been possible to describe here the variations in average height between different occupations, which offer an intriguing supplement to the evidence of real wage rates. Other data sources, such as the records of prisons, of the East India company, and of the Royal and merchant navies, still remain to be exploited. The growing volume of research on heights in other countries of Europe and in north America makes it increasingly possible to see Britain within a wider context.

There are, of course, many problems of interpretation. Just because nutritional status, and thus height, is a measure which sums up so much in the environment, it can often be difficult to link a particular change in height to a particular cause. Human biologists differ, also, in their views on the ages which are most crucial in setting children on a particular growth path. It is not clear how much trauma or improvement is required in childhood or in adolescence to disturb the path on which the child set out in infancy.

Despite these problems, the evidence of nutritional status which is provided by height data offers an intriguing new way to approach an old, but not yet exhausted, topic. The standard of living debate will run and run.

REFERENCES AND FURTHER READING

(1) **N. F. R. Crafts,** 'The Industrial Revolution: Economic Growth in Britain, 1700–1860', *ReFRESH*, 4 (Spring 1987). Reprinted as Chapter 5 in this volume.
(2) **M. W. Flinn (ed.),** *Report on the Sanitary Condition of the Labouring Population by Edwin Chadwick* (Edinburgh, 1965).
(3) **E. J. Hobsbawm and R. M. Hartwell,** 'The Standard of Living during the Industrial Revolution: A Discussion', *Economic History Review,* XVI (1963).
(4) **P. Mathias,** 'Preface' to Taylor [5].
(5) **A. J. Taylor (ed.),** *The Standard of Living in Britain in the Industrial Revolution* (London, 1975).

10 Women and Society: Continuity and Change since 1870

J. LEWIS

Given the well-documented absence of women from most of the basic history texts, it is easy to understand why female historians in particular have felt the need to explore women's past. However, there has been relatively little cross-fertilisation between this work and other types of history, which makes it difficult to integrate the history of women into more general interpretations in modern history. Ideally, there should be discussion of the experience of women, as well as men, in the treatment of subjects such as work experience or the effects of social welfare provision.

EVALUATING CHANGE

In practice, assessing the specifics of women's position in modern society poses problems, however, since this necessarily involves looking at the legal, social, economic, and political factors contributing to 'women's emancipation' or the 'improvement of women's status'. But the changes in women's position over time are not nearly as cut and dried as such labelling implies. For while few of us, male or female, would relish a return to the kind of material conditions experienced by the majority of the late-nineteenth-century population, it is nevertheless impossible to see the history of women in terms of straightforward progress towards 'emancipation'. Ivy Pinchbeck's classic account, *Women Workers in the Industrial Revolution, 1750–1850* (1930) was optimistic in its interpretations. She viewed the gradual emergence of a family wage

130

and the increasing specialisation of male and female roles into breadwinner and housewife as a progressive development, emancipating women from the burden of waged labour and bringing them more leisure and greater comfort, as well as enabling them to pursue the childbearing and household tasks she believed them to be best fitted for. In 1931 only 11 per cent of married women worked: indeed, it was not until 1961 that the economic activity rate for women (excluding those in unpaid domestic work) again reached the level recorded in the 1861 Census (see Table 10). Feminists, and in all probability a majority of the 58 per cent of the married women who work today, would not only reject Pinchbeck's idea as to what constitutes progress and emancipation but would also point out the astonishing continuity in the degree of sexual segregation in the work place and in the ratio between women's and men's pay.

It is essential to come to some balanced assessment of the continuity and change in women's position, and to question the idea that change can be seen in terms of simple linear progress. Furthermore, changes in one area of women's lives that effected greater equality between the sexes were not necessarily accompanied by similar progress in other areas. Nor should the experience of single and married women, or of working- and middle-class women be conflated. Thus, while it is true that the range of occupations open to women increased at the end of the nineteenth century, this did not affect the number of married women in the work force, and not until after the First World War was it usual for middle-class girls to work before marriage. Similarly, in respect to women's reproductive experience (one of the most important determinants of health status for women), middle-class women were having smaller families by the late nineteenth century, but working-class family size did not show a significant fall until the inter-war period. Even then contemporary surveys show that working-class married women reported as much disabling illness at the end of the 1930s as they did just before the First World War.

In line with the initial desire to make women visible, a number of historians have explored aspects of nineteenth- and twentieth-century feminism. In her book *Faces of Feminism* [1] Olive Banks has identified three strands of feminism: the evangelical, equal rights, and socialist. But this is too tidy a schema properly to encompass the complex nature of feminist ideas and behaviour. For example, both Josephine Butler, an evangelical feminist, and Millicent Fawcett, an equal rights feminist, made use of the arguments of Victorian Darwinistic science that most women's talents were primarily domestic, to press for an extension of these virtues to the wider sphere beyond the home.

It is common for the influence of feminism to be questioned. For example, the increased attention paid to the education of middle-class girls during the late Victorian period is seen by some to be as much the result of the general educational reform initiative of the period as of feminist ambition, and the contribution of the suffrage movement to securing the vote has long been an issue for debate. But we should be wary of judging the importance of nineteenth- and early-twentieth-century feminism too narrowly. In her book *Girls Growing Up* ... [2] Carol Dyhouse has argued powerfully that the new endowed and proprietary girls' schools, of which there were 200 by 1894, provided girls with different role models and access to a peer group. It also succeeded in loosening family ties. Similarly the suffrage movement succeeded in keeping the vote on the political agenda in the face of an extensive and sometimes misogynist opposition.

It is a matter of debate as to how important legislative reform has been in changing the position of women. As long ago as the 1950s, Richard Titmuss suggested that changes in patterns of pregnancy and childbirth were much more important for explaining changes in women's position in society than the acquisition of legal rights. (The changing trends in fertility are charted in Figure 8.) Most of the recent literature on women's history has focused on women's experience of production and reproduction in recognition of the importance of these factors. But it is possible to be overly dismissive of the legal framework within which women lived their lives; in the nineteenth century married women had no legal personality and no capacity to enter into contracts in the market place. When taken together with scientific and evangelical ideas as to the female character, capacity and place, this in large measure accounts for the acute separation of spheres experienced by middle-class women in particular. We are only just beginning to explore the effects that lack of access to divorce, and the legal obligation to provide household and sexual services to husbands, had on the meaning of marriage for women.

HOME AND FAMILY

Some of the most exciting recent work in the field has sought to reconstruct women's (particularly working-class women's)

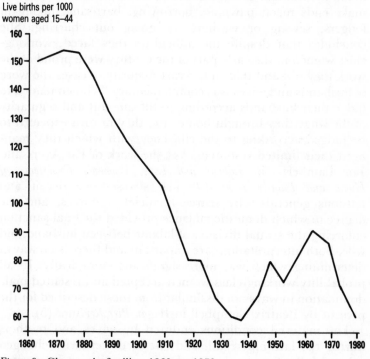

Figure 8 Changes in fertility, 1860s to 1970s

133

experience of home and family. It is difficult to write about any inarticulate group, and many historians of women have employed the new techniques of oral history to good effect for the recent past. When interviews are used in conjunction with material from autobiographies, contemporary social surveys (such as those by Booth and Rowntree), commentaries by social investigators (such as M. S. Pember Reeves and M. Spring Rice), and census data, we can begin to build up a picture of working-class life. This view is considerably more realistic than that offered by some sociologists, who see husband/wife relationships developing smoothly from the sexually segregated to the 'symmetrical', and mother/child relationships moving from neglectful to caring.

It is nevertheless possible for historians looking at similar evidence to arrive at very different interpretations. Elizabeth Roberts' recent book *A Woman's Place* [3] describes in vivid detail the number of strategies women resorted to in order to make ends meet: pawning, borrowing, bartering, taking in lodgers, sewing or washing, or going out charring. She concludes that despite the difficulties they faced, working-class women in the early part of the century were proud of the work they did and that in the vast majority of cases the work of husbands and wives was complementary. Women tended to judge their husbands according to the amount and regularity of the wage they brought home, and they in turn expected to be judged according to the efficiency with which they managed their limited resources. Yet the work of Pat Ayers and Jan Lambertz in *Labour and Love. Women's Experience of Home and Family 1850–1940* [4], stresses the deceit and tensions generated by scarce financial resources, and the degree to which domestic violence provided the final sanction enforcing the sexual division of labour between husband and wife. Both interpretations are important and there is no way of determining which was more significant numerically. In all probability working-class women accepted and resented male domination in ways not dissimilar from those described for the present by Beatrix Campbell in *Wigan Pier Revisited* (5).

The material conditions endured by wives and mothers during the late nineteenth and twentieth centuries changed substantially for the better. During the inter-war period, working-class wives of regularly employed men could begin to cook by gas and think about moving to a house with a bathroom on a new estate. For middle-class women it is possible that the modern suburban house of the inter-war years, better equipped with labour-saving devices, with either a resident servant or daily help and a small number of children, provided women with more leisure than either the large household staffs of the Victorian period or the usually servantless houses of the post-Second World War years. Most important was the decline in family size. As the maternity letters collected by the Women's Cooperative Guild just before the First World War show so movingly, women's ignorance of their bodies and inability to obtain access to either contraceptives or the privacy necessary for the practice of female methods of birth control, led to frequent pregnancies and extraordinary suffering. Recent work has put forward a number of reasons for the increasing use of contraception, which resulted in the decline in the birth rate known as 'the demographic transition', beginning around 1870 (see Figure 8). Opinion is divided between those who emphasise women's determination to exercise their right to 'voluntary mother-hood', and those who attribute prime importance to men's desire to limit their families in order to achieve the 'paraphernalia of gentility' and upward career mobility for themselves and their sons. In all probability, family size was negotiated between husband and wife. In her study of the inter-war decline of working-class family size, *Fair Sex* [6], Diana Gittins has concluded that couples whose lives centred on the increasingly privatised world of the home, rather than on the culture of the work place or on the spouses' respective circles of friends, most frequently achieved their ideal family size.

EMPLOYMENT OUTSIDE THE HOME

It has been a major contribution of the new women's history to point out the links between family and work experiences. For example, women's traditionally weak participation in trade unions should be understood in relation to the way in which young women's relationship to unions and the work

135

place was mediated by female kin, who often found their first jobs and paid their union dues. In other words, the young female worker had an indirect relationship to her union and work place. Early-twentieth-century writers often noted that women appeared to accept the idea of a woman's job and a woman's rate, apparently in anticipation of the fact that they would marry and become dependent on a male 'family wage'.

It is clear that male and female workers, as well as policy-makers, believed in the concept of a family wage as an ideal. It can be argued that trade-union struggles for a family wage benefited working-class families to the extent that it raised the wages of the male breadwinner. However, the struggle was conducted at the expense of the woman worker and, within the family, the family wage system benefited men to the extent that they gained the privilege of being served at home by their wives. In addition, to the extent that the family wage was never realised, women were forced to shoulder the double burden of household and paid employment. At the same time they received little assistance from government welfare legislation, such as national insurance, which assumed female economic dependency to be the norm.

Throughout the late nineteenth and early twentieth centuries, it was believed to be more respectable for married women not to work. Indeed, labour historians have begun to acknowledge the role played by wives in achieving 'respectability'. Visible manifestations of respectability included whitened doorsteps and a 'clean' rent book, although in the context of primitive domestic tchnology and unpredictable income, such things were hard to achieve. Single women were also often anxious to work in 'respectable' occupations; this meant that warehouse work, though low paid, was much preferred to machine work because it was light and clean. As Sidney Webb commented in 1891, 'for women's work the "gentility" of the occupation is still accepted as part payment'.

The range of opportunities during the nineteenth century for women's paid work was confined largely to textile manufacturing and domestic service. It was only with the changes in the structure of occupations during the last quarter of the century that the number of (primarily single) working women increased (see Table 10). The number of women engaged in

Table 10   Female participation in the labour force in
Great Britain, 1861–1981

	Working Women as % of all women[a]			Women as % of total labour force[b]
	Single	Married	Total	
1861	,,	,,	42	31
1871	,,	,,	42	31
1881	,,	,,	39	30
1891	,,	,,	38	30
1901	,,	,,	36	29
1911	66	10	37	29
1921	67	9	36	29
1931	70	11	37	30
1951	72	24	40	31
1961	77	34	46	33
1971	70	49	55	37
1981	69	57	61	39

[a] Covers women aged 15–64 for 1861–1951; 15–60 for 1961–71; and
16–60 for 1981.
[b] All ages.

Source: *Census of Population.*

'white blouse' work (mainly teaching, retailing, office work
and nursing) increased 161 per cent between 1881 and 1911.
Nevertheless, some form of domestic service was still the
single largest employer of women as late as 1931. The
expansion of jobs for women during the First World War
achieved no lasting effect. But women's consciousness *was*
changed by their wartime experiences: autobiographies as
different as those of Vera Brittain for the First World War
and Nella Last (the wife of a Barrow fitter), for the Second
World War, show that neither was able comfortably to settle
back into their previous stultifying domestic routines.

To this day women's work remains characteristically low-
paid and sexually segregated from that of men. Even in textiles,
where women traditionally received equal pay for equal work,
they rarely earned the same, because they worked fewer
hours, had fewer looms, and were not considered able to tune

137

and adjust their own looms. In 1906 the average wage for all adult women textile workers was 15/5d, on the borderline of what was reckoned to be the minimum subsistence for a single woman. The average wage for women over 18 in all other industries was 12/11d.

There are very few general accounts of women's work available, and there is considerable debate – more frequently between sociologists than historians – about the causes of women's low pay and low status. There is no doubt that male craft unions tended to exclude women workers, and that professional associations dominated by men also did so for occupations such as medicine. But employers and women themselves also shared firm ideas as to what work was appropriate for women and what women were capable of. Women's position in the labour market can only be explained by the complex changes between women and men workers, trade unions, employers and the state, and in relation to the changing nature and structure of jobs, which is in turn dependent on the scale and technique of production and methods of work organisation. Given that their work experience and expectations have been largely confined to unskilled work or monotonous clerical tasks (indeed skilled work has become by definition work that is not performed by women), it is understandable that women should have thought of their paid employment as secondary, to be undertaken at the dictates of the family economy. In their useful summary volume, *Women, Work and Family* [7], Louise Tilly and Joan Scott have described women in the twentieth century as moving towards a more individualistic position and working for their own satisfaction. It is doubtful whether this has ever happened for the majority of unskilled, poorly paid women workers.

ACTIVISTS OR VICTIMS

The major interpretative issue running through all the recent literature on women's history is the extent to which women may be regarded as 'victims' – at the hands of the state, male trade unionists, and husbands – or as active agents, controlling their own fate. Part of the problem in evaluating this stems from the fact that historians of women are often forced to rely on prescriptive literature such as domestic manuals and infant care handbooks as source material, and it is often difficult to assess how far these dictated or reflected contemporary behaviour. In the case of nineteenth-century, middle-class women, the traditional picture of the passive, idle 'angel of the house' portrayed as the ideal in contemporary literature, and accepted uncritically in many history texts, has been subjected to searching enquiry of late. This is not to deny that women still undertook mindless and time-consuming rituals, such as calling and card leaving but, as Leonore Davidoff has shown in *The Best Circles* [8] it would be wrong to interpret these as having no purpose. Just as working-class women were guardians of domestic respectability, so women in middle-class households were responsible for maintaining the differentiation between new and old wealth.

Middle-class women's lives are not today narrowly confined to the domestic sphere, and working-class women no longer perform hard household labour and undergo frequent pregnancies in addition to taking on paid work, as and when the family economy demands it. Since the Second World War, dwindling numbers of domestic servants and a more general ownership of household appliances, together with smaller families have acted as levellers in terms of women's experience of home and family. Furthermore, since the war there has been a revolution in terms of married women's participation in the labour market. Shirley Conran's prescription for 'Superwoman' – the middle-class woman who holds down a professional job, entertains and keeps house with maximum efficiency – could not be more different from the prescriptions meted out to nineteenth-century, middle-class women. Significantly, it is still women who are expected to take primary responsibility for the domestic sphere and they are still found in low-paid, low-status jobs.

In seeking to weigh the relative importance of continuity against change, socio-economic against legislative factors, or the portrayal of women as victims or active agents, it may help to consider possible lifecycle experiences of women in a particular social class for a specific historical period. For in

Illustration 5 A suffragette view of women's votes

my view, it helps to see changes in educational opportunities, prescriptive beliefs, legal impediments, employment structure, health status and the rest as the boundaries within which women have acted. We could, for example, take the early-twentieth-century experience of Francie Nicol (told by Joe Robinson in the *Life and Times of Francie Nicol of South Shields*) to whom painful childbirth and a drunken husband are to be endured, and hard times expected. The limitations imposed on Francie by class, poverty, a poor education, ignorance of her own body and marital dependency are clear to an observer. Yet she behaves with unlimited vitality and resourcefulness, opening a fish and chip shop to support her children, and when her husband returns to drink away the profits, starting again. Today there is easier access to divorce, birth control and state welfare benefits are more readily available, and yet a majority of single mothers still find themselves trapped by their sole responsibility for child care, by their poverty and their lack of marketable skills.

The illustration comes from the period of the suffragette campaigns yet possesses a broader significance than this since the message is still pertinent today. Over the past century women have benefited from a wide variety of changes, yet boundaries still exist to limit their activity and shape their potential.

REFERENCES AND FURTHER READING

(1) **O. Banks,** *Faces of Feminism* (Oxford, 1981).
(2) **C. Dyhouse,** *Girls Growing Up in Late Victorian and Edwardian England* (London, 1981).
(3) **E. Roberts,** *A Woman's Place. An Oral History of Working-Class Women, 1890–1940* (Oxford, 1984).
(4) **J. Lewis** (ed.), *Labour and Love. Women's Experience of Home and Family 1850–1940* (Oxford, 1987).
(5) **B. Campbell,** *Wigan Pier Revisited* (London, 1984).
(6) **D. Gittins,** *Fair Sex. Family Size and Structure, 1900–39* (London, 1982).
(7) **L. Tilly and J. Scott,** *Women, Work, and Family* (London, 1978).
(8) **L. Davidoff,** *The Best Circles* (London, 1973).

(9) **S. Lewenhak,** *Women and Trade Unions* (London, 1977).

(10) **A. V. John** (ed.), *Unequal Opportunities: Women's Employment in England 1800–1918* (Oxford, 1986).

(11) **J. Rendall** (ed.), *Equal or Different: Women's Politics 1800–1914* (Oxford, 1987).

(12) **J. Weeks,** *Sex, Politics, and Society: The Regulation of Sexuality since 1800* (London, 1981).

11 The British Welfare State: Its Origins and Character

P. Thane

We should be clear about what we mean by a 'welfare state'. As conventionally used in the years since 1945, when it became part of our everyday vocabulary, it means a state which defines as an essential part of its role the maintenance of a reasonable standard of life for all its citizens. The state may seek to achieve this broad goal by a variety of means including provision of cash benefits and/or services, tax relief under the fiscal system, and the regulation of the labour market. Indeed, a high proportion of the activities of the modern state has some welfare content.

Over the past century such activities have certainly grown in size, range and cost. But the causes and consequences of such growth are complex. It is clearer if we analyse this process separately from the related question of whether living standards of the population improved; a topic addressed by Roderick Floud in Chapter 9. The precise role of state welfare in relation to other agencies such as the family, or voluntary or private institutions, in bringing about these improvements is also best considered as a distinct subject. Whilst these processes are obviously related it should not be assumed that they progress naturally together. It is also helpful to bear in mind that although state welfare measures may have been intended to raise general standards of welfare, they did not always do so. Neither was this always their sole purpose. And the fact that the present-day state performs more welfare functions than in the past does not necessarily imply that it has displaced other agencies as providers of welfare. Rather their roles may have grown side by side. Finally, it is salutary to see

143

that the intended consequences of social legislation are often not the same as the actual results.

PRESSURES FOR CHANGES IN WELFARE FROM THE 1870S

By 1880 central and local government were responsible for a significant range of welfare functions. The poor law was the most important agency in providing a framework of benefits and services for those in acute need [Rose (1)]. From the 1870s it provided institutionalised care, of an increasingly specialised and less punitive character, for a growing range of people in need: the sick, the elderly, and orphaned or abandoned children. However, the reasons for the growth of institutional care at this time remain unclear, and need further investigation [Crowther (2)].

At the same time that the administrators of the poor-law system were seeking to expand institutional provision for the helpless poor, they also sought to cut back cash benefits in the form of outdoor relief to people in their own homes. Where possible, the aim was to transfer responsibility for maintenance outside the workhouse to the family, to charity or to employers. In this way they hoped at last to realise the objectives of the New Poor Law of 1834 and to abolish outdoor allowances to the able-bodied poor. But the central poor-law authorities had difficulty in imposing such uniformity of policy on local administrators – the boards of guardians. These boards retained considerable independence, had unequal resources to draw on in the form of income from the poor rates, and were confronted by diverse problems. Local variations in practice therefore remained. In the long term, however, such diversity decreased as a result of central pressure. This illustrates an important theme in the history of social policy during the past century – the steady tightening of central control over local government.

From the 1880s central government came under increasing pressure to extend its welfare functions outside the poor law, and in part this resulted from the activities of the poor-law administrators themselves. As institutional provision for such 'deserving' groups as the sick improved, it seemed less obvious

144

why they should remain within the unpopular framework of a deterrent poor law. The cuts in outdoor relief also caused hardship to others traditionally regarded as 'deserving', such as old people and single parent families. The family and voluntary agencies could not entirely replace the former public provision so that greater destitution ensued. This was not necessarily because families were unwilling to give support to needy kin. Some were simply too poor themselves to be able to help. And many of the elderly poor had no kin; some had never married, some were childless, whilst others had children who had emigrated or died. Where kin were present there is strong evidence that they were a principal source of support for those in need. In addition, charity from the rich, or not so rich, might also help a little. But despite the large sums that were given, the enlarged demands on charitable funds were so great that they proved inadequate to meet growing needs.

The resulting intensification of hardship among the elderly poor was an important reason for a growing demand for state old age pensions from the late 1870s onwards. There was no similar demand until around the time of the First World War for cash benefits, in the form of family allowances, for mothers and children. Their treatment by the poor law was just one of a very wide range of pressures on the government to make new forms of provision for infants, children, and their mothers at the end of the nineteenth century.

Concern about the physical debility of the British population – with pressure on the state to take remedial action – is often dated from the discovery of the poor physical condition of recruits to the army during the Boer War of 1899–1902. Though such concern was intensified by these wartime discoveries, it had been evident for the two previous decades. Fears were expressed that generations of urban living, in often appalling conditions, were leading to degeneration of the national physique. Commentators pointed to the fact that Britain was the most urbanised society in the world with nine out of ten of its population living in towns and cities. Fears about what was construed as national decline were intensified by continuing high infant mortality, and by a falling birth rate after 1870. The decrease in family size was fastest amongst the better-off, whom it was assumed were the physically fittest specimens in the 'national stock'. These anxieties were the more acute at a time when Britain faced growing overseas competition economically and imperially. It was therefore seen as very important to nurture fit workers and soldiers for present and future needs.

ATTITUDES TO EXPANDED STATE WELFARE

As a result of these and other pressures, demands were made from the 1880s for central and local governments to improve housing and sanitation; to assist in the provision of cheap milk to mothers and young children; to supply medical care and meals in schools; and to protect children against cruelty and neglect. By the end of the century this had some effect in the shape of national legislation, and local authority or voluntary action. But opposition came from those who still believed in minimal state intervention in the life of the family. This included poor families themselves who often resented what they saw as official interference in their lives. At the same time the poor might be grateful for *positive* help. The 30 to 40 per cent of the population (or more), who could expect at some point in their lives to experience hardship, had complicated attitudes to state welfare. From 1867 the extension of the franchise at local and national level to include significant numbers of working-class males and, at local level, numbers of women also, undoubtedly increased demand for more and better provision by the state of education, housing, health care, and protection against unemployment. It also strengthened the belief among politicians that if such provision was not made working-class political organisation would grow.

Not all working people, even in the emerging Labour Party, supported a major and permanent welfare role for the state. Many of them gave higher priority to the state taking on the role of regulating the labour market to ensure full employment and adequate wages. This would have the merit of enabling more people to practise self-help and escape from the low pay and underemployment that were major causes of their poverty. At best this could be a long-term aim and, in the shorter term, they recognised that only the state had the resources to relieve the scale of need well known to working people. The extent of that poverty was revealed to a wider audience by Charles Booth's survey of London (published in full in 1902) and Seebohm Rowntree's survey of York (published in 1901).

EDWARDIAN POLITICS AND WELFARE LEGISLATION

There were contradictory influences upon ministries at the turn of the twentieth century, either to ignore the 'social problem', or to remedy it by varied collectivist action. The Conservatives, who were in office from 1895 to 1905, made only a limited response since they were inhibited by opposition among their supporters to any increase in taxation in the interests of the poor. The Liberals, who succeeded them, were similarly constrained because: they were the party of free trade and low taxation; they included an 'old' Liberal wing antagonistic to social reform; and they were also conscious of the hostility to social reform of the Conservative-dominated House of Lords. In consequence the social measures that the Liberals introduced were neither costly to the Exchequer nor notably redistributive. Impelling them into social reform, however, was an influential 'New Liberal' wing which believed that the state, and a Liberal government in particular, should act to remedy social conditions for reasons of principle rather than for political calculation. However, political considerations also played their part. To a greater extent than the Conservatives, the Liberals were dependent upon the working-class vote and were concerned about the attractiveness of the Labour Party to it. These political considerations are evident in campaigning Liberal material. (See Illustrations 6 and 7.) Both the strengths and weaknesses of the legislation that was enacted are explained by these tensions.

The earliest reforms enacted at the time of the Liberal ministry owed relatively little to the New Liberalism. The first enactment – the provision of free school meals in 1906 – was in fact introduced by a Labour MP. And the introduction of medical inspection in schools in the following year was essentially the work of civil servants making the first moves

147

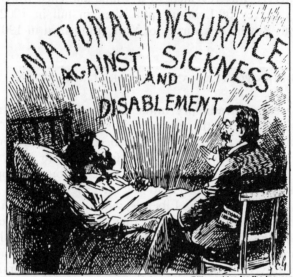

THE DAWN OF HOPE.

Mr. LLOYD GEORGE'S National Health Insurance Bill provides for the insurance of the Worker in case of Sickness.

Support the Liberal Government
in their policy of
SOCIAL REFORM.

Illustration 6 Political capital extracted from the National Insurance Act, 1911

towards a national free medical service [Gilbert (3)]. (This illustrates the importance of civil servants in welfare policy-making; in this case a constructive role was played, although in other instances they were sometimes obstructive.) The Liberals themselves initiated old age pensions in 1908. This was the product of a long campaign and was the first cash benefit to be paid by the state outside the poor law. Nonetheless it at first imposed on claimants means and character tests not far removed in spirit from the poor law. The Children Act of the same year was a response to thirty years of lobbying for the comprehensive state protection of children. The Trades

THE TWO OLD AGE
PENSION RECORDS

I.–The TORY RECORD

1895.—Tory Government returned to power pledged to give Old Age Pensions. The promise of Old Age Pensions was the most attractive item in the "Social Programme" put forward by Mr. Chamberlain in 1894 and "fully approved" by the Tory leader (the late Lord Salisbury) before the General Election of 1895.

1895–1905.—Tories in power for a period of ten years. **Nothing done,** except the appointment of one Commission and three Committees to enquire into the question. Subject suddenly discovered to be not in Mr. Chamberlain's Department!

II.–The LIBERAL RECORD

1906 (Jan.).—Liberal Government returned to power unpledged to give Old Age Pensions.

1906 (Nov.).—"The matter will be dealt with as soon as time and money permit." (SIR H. CAMPBELL-BANNERMAN.)

1907.—A definite sum set aside as a "nest egg" for Old Age Pensions. "It is our intention, before the close of the next Session of this Parliament, to lay firm the foundations of this Reform." (MR. ASQUITH.)

1908.—**Old Age Pensions Act Passed.**

1909.—Pensions paid from New Year's Day to pensioners of over 70, nearly all getting 5/- a week.

1911.—Poor Law Relief Disqualification came to an end on January 1st **The number of pensioners raised to over 900,000 at a cost of nearly 12½ millions a year.**

Study these Two Records and you will soon see which is the Better of the Two.

Published by the LIBERAL PUBLICATION DEPARTMENT (in connection with the National Liberal Federation and the Liberal Central Association, 42 Parliament Street, S.W., and Printed by Page & Thomas, Ltd., Chesham.
LEAFLET NO. 2390]   24.7.11.   [Price 2s. per 1000.

Illustration 7 Welfare and electoral advantage: the Old Age Pensions Act, 1908

Boards Act of 1909 introduced a minimum wage and improved conditions for some of the lowest paid, and largely female occupations. The Housing and Town Planning Act of the same year sought to limit existing and future urban overcrowding and pollution. Successive Lloyd George budgets rendered the system of direct taxation somewhat more progressive. National insurance, introduced in 1911, provided health and unemployment benefits for the regularly employed, in return for compulsory weekly contributions that were designed to relieve the Treasury of a considerable burden. Social insurance was also intended to build long-established values into a state venture; the regular payment reminded the worker of the obligation of self-help and saving, and established for him – or more rarely her – a contractual right to benefit.

Collectively this was a significant leap in the state's responsibility for welfare and established new principles of lasting importance. But the principles involved were various and lacked co-ordination since they were the product of the diverse pressures of preceding decades. It is important to appreciate that there was no underlying intention to establish the state as the permanent primary provider of welfare. On the one hand, it was intended to rescue deserving groups such as the elderly poor from the poor law. On the other hand, measures (such as the Trades Board, and National Insurance Acts), began a process of providing for the bulk of the non-pauper working population a basic security against destitution – seen as undeserved because it was due to low pay, sickness or unemployment. On this basis they could then practise self-help more effectively.

These measures were limited, tentative and almost immediately faced pressure for improvement. Their effects are hard to assess because of the onset of the First World War. The war extended the range of state responsibilities in social and economic matters, and popular expectations of collectivism were correspondingly heightened. Living standards improved due, above all, to full wartime employment [Winter (4)], and with this rose general expectations about the future. The influence of the Labour Party increased. Fear of post-war disorder – should popular hopes be dashed – influenced the wartime government in making plans for post-war reconstruction. And at the end of the war the franchise was greatly extended, with long-term implications for the provision of welfare.

THE INTER-WAR YEARS

Some wartime legislation outlived the war. This included maternity and child welfare measures, since awareness of the large number of war dead made it even more necessary to protect the future 'national' stock. Among reconstruction proposals only the more politically urgent were implemented. Education and housing legislation, introduced in 1918 and 1919, had only qualified impact since their scope was reduced after the onset of depression in 1920. But the planned extension of unemployment benefit to virtually all manual workers was not cut back, in view of the growing numbers of unemployed.

Until recently the inter-war years have been treated somewhat cursorily in the historiography of welfare. They were seen as having been dominated by the outstanding social problem of unemployment. And the central fact of welfare administration has been perceived as the meanness with which the unemployed were treated. Yet, for all the shifts in policy and failings of generosity, the administration of benefit was a considerable achievement and unthinkable at any previous time. It was provided on a regular basis at subsistence level to unprecedented numbers of people, over a period of twenty years. In itself it marked a significant and lasting shift in the acknowledged responsibilities of the state to its citizens.

The costs of unemployment relief may have diverted expenditure from other areas of social welfare, whilst unemployment itself created additional social problems. It is difficult to argue, however, that conditions in the depressed areas were worse than anything that had been experienced before 1914. A more accurate interpretation would suggest that severe poverty could sometimes afflict different districts and occupational groups more comprehensively than before. And fewer people

151

appeared willing to tolerate hardship for themselves and others as an avoidable fact of life. But governments were still reluctant to acknowledge the effects of unemployment in malnutrition and ill-health [Webster (5)].

Yet in other respects welfare provision became more comprehensive during the inter-war years. In 1925 the national insurance system was expanded to include pensions for those aged from 65 to 70, and for widows and orphans. There was notable expansion in educational provision, in council-house building, and in local-authority hospitals. Much of this depended on local-authority initiative and the availability of adequate financial resources. Poorer districts had long been hampered by their low rate income, but were now increasingly subsidised by central government, which saw this as the only way to expand and equalise expensive services such as housing. Combined with a growing strength of the Labour Party in urban local government, this sustained innovation at the local level. These factors also led central government – notably during Neville Chamberlain's period as Minister of Health from 1925 to 1929 – to strengthen its control over localities, as in the Local Government Act of 1929. The Act transferred many of the 'caring' functions of the poor law to county and municipal authorities. Its residual responsibilities for the relief of destitution remained until 1948, so that the poor law continued to deal with social casualties for whom no other services existed.

The inter-war period was one of significant change and expansion in the welfare responsibilities of the state. This was not the outcome of any plan, despite a vogue for planning in the 1930s. From a variety of such schemes to ease Britain out of depression came the seeds of much of the social legislation introduced after 1945.

WARTIME AND POST-WAR MEASURES

It was not planning but war that ended economic depression. The period from 1939 to 1945 brought about a renewed expansion of state activities; a certain levelling of living standards; a succession of government plans for a better post-war world; and a popular desire not to return to inter-war conditions. That war induced an enhanced sense of social cohesion or changed social relationships significantly is, in my view, doubtful. But in the short run both wars created in government a sense of obligation to those who had suffered. War also brought about sufficient change to make it impossible to turn the clock back to a pre-war world, as those who wished to do so in 1918 had found. The pressures for change were much stronger at the end of the Second World War; the wartime government introduced the Education Act in 1944 and family allowances in 1945. Substantial social legislation was expected whether the Conservatives or Labour won the general election in 1945.

In 1945 the electoral victors – the first majority Labour government – were committed to change, although there was little sign of a coherent long-term strategy or of ideological distinctiveness in their legislative programme. Much of it was built on earlier proposals and especially those of a Liberal, W. H. Beveridge. Its chief characteristic was a commitment to universal provision where appropriate (as with education, health and national insurance), in order to make available to the whole community the benefits previously reserved in practice for manual workers. Cash benefits were paid at a minimal level, due mainly to the troubles of the economy. Labour also significantly pushed forward the pre-war trend towards increased central control over local government. If there was a unifying aim it was the long-run liberal ideal of equalising opportunity. Significant space remained for self-help (e.g. in the private provision of medical care), voluntary action, and family support (promoted as vigorously by this, as by previous ministries). An unintended result of this expansion of social welfare was that the relatively better-off benefited significantly from such universalised and improved services as health and education. Also unforeseen was that the high proportion of pensioners who were wholly dependent upon public funds were able to subsist only with the aid of National Assistance – the stigmatising and selective successor to the poor law established in 1948.

153

Overall, however, there was distinctly less primary poverty after the Second World War than before, as there had been less in 1918 than in 1914. The reason for the higher levels of peacetime prosperity than had been known previously was less the existence of the welfare state than that of full employment in the later 1940s and 1950s. Full employment was itself a welfare objective of the wartime and post-war ministries but its achievement owed much more to world economic conditions than to government plans. Viewed from the 1980s it is apparent that welfare measures in themselves have a very limited capacity to effect social change. That post-war government overestimated the degree to which welfare policies could narrow social inequalities was because nothing so ambitious had ever been tried before.

Poverty surveys from Booth to Townsend [Townsend (6)] suggest that patterns of social inequality have changed little over this century. This does not mean that the emergence of a welfare state has had no effect. Rather it implies that the effect of this vast machine has been to keep society stable. It has brought about no marked change in the distribution of wealth or power, but has prevented those who have not benefited individually from the enormous growth in national affluence during the last century from falling too dangerously far behind the living standards of the rest.

REFERENCES AND FURTHER READING

(1) **M. E. Rose,** *The Relief of Poverty 1834–1914* (London, second edn, 1986).
(2) **M. A. Crowther,** *Social Policy in Britain, 1914–39* (London, 1988).
(3) **B. B. Gilbert,** *The Evolution of National Insurance in Great Britain* (London, 1960).
(4) **J. M. Winter,** *The Great War and the British People* (London, 1985).
(5) **C. Webster,** 'Health, Welfare and Unemployment during the Depression', *Past and Present*, 109 (1985).
(6) **P. Townsend,** *Poverty in the United Kingdom* (Harmondsworth, 1979).
(7) **A. Digby,** *British Welfare Policy: Workhouse to Workforce* (Faber, 1989).

IV Labour

12 Chartism

E. ROYLE

The nature of Chartism has been the subject of controversy since the earliest days of the Charter. When J. R. Stephens told a vast audience on Kersal Moor, Manchester, in 1838 that 'This question of Universal Suffrage was a knife and fork question' he came close to denying that Chartism was primarily a political movement at all. By contrast William Lovett and the members of the London Working Men's Association who drafted the Charter in 1837 were staunch believers in democracy and the inalienable natural rights of man. Both views embodied strong ideological perspectives: Stephens was a Tory; Lovett a radical. Whilst recognising the truth in both positions, the majority of historians until recently have inclined towards the Stephens interpretation that the Chartist movement was based upon the social and economic grievances of the people. The more political interpretation was given new vigour with the publication of Edward Thompson's *Making of the English Working Class* in 1963, since when attention has turned to the 'political culture' of the Chartist experience. This has entailed a reconsideration of the causes of early Chartist growth, the organisational activities of the 1840s, the role of Feargus O'Connor and the significance of his Land Plan, the nature of rank-and-file support (including that of women), and the reasons for Chartist failure.

THE TRADITIONAL INTERPRETATION

A close connection between economic circumstances and the varying fortunes of Chartism has long been recognised. The mass movement flourished in the 'Hungry Forties' depression

157

of 1837–42 and briefly revived in the depression of 1847–8. Local studies have confirmed the appeal of Chartism in areas of dying industry such as Wiltshire, and among declining trades such as handloom weaving [Briggs (1)]. Such a view goes beyond crude economic determinism, though. As Disraeli said in the parliamentary debate on the Charter in 1839, 'where there were economical causes for national movements they led to tumult but seldom to organisation'. Quite clearly Chartism was organised. In Disraeli's opinion the real cause of Chartism was the conduct of Whig governments after 1830 and the false philosophy of their utilitarian allies. In this he was at one with Thomas Carlyle and, indeed, J. R. Stephens. Legislation such as the Poor Law Amendment Act of 1834 had deprived the people of their 'civil rights'. In this form the tory-social explanation for Chartism has become orthodoxy for a wide spectrum of historians in the twentieth century. As G. D. H. Cole observed in *Chartist Portraits* (1941): 'Hunger and hatred – these were the forces that made Chartism a mass movement of the British working class'.

Alongside this economic and social view of the mass movement developed an account of the political leadership which was scarcely flattering. The main source for this view is the collection of papers put together by Francis Place, whose career spanned radicalism from the London Corresponding Society in the 1790s to the London Working Men's Association and beyond. Place saw Chartism not as a mass movement at all, but as a political pressure group working to persuade the electors and to educate the non-electors in the need for democracy. He resented the way in which a movement which he had nurtured in its earliest days had been perverted from its rational and peaceful course by a mass movement of irrational and violent anti-Poor Law protesters led by Feargus O'Connor. This view, embodied in the Place Papers in the British Library, was confirmed by other evidence readily available to historians, notably the earliest *History* of the Chartist movement by R. G. Gammage (1854), whose hero, Bronterre O'Brien, had quarrelled with O'Connor in 1841; and the autobiography of William Lovett, which naturally enhanced his own reputation at the expense of that of the man with whom he most profoundly disagreed.

The resulting synthesis of these views was an interpretation of Chartism as a mass social and economic movement of local grievances with a political programme furnished by respectable artisan radicals, thwarted by the wild ambitions of an unscrupulous demagogue. The reasons for the failure of Chartism were thus not hard to find. They lay partly in an improvement in economic conditions which undermined the mass movement as early as 1842, and partly in bad leadership, weak organisation and the irresponsible tactic of violent language. And the most culpable leader was O'Connor.

REINTERPRETATIONS – ORIGINS

Disraeli also argued that, 'Political rights had so much of an abstract character, their consequences acted so slightly on the multitude', that he did not believe they could ever be the origin of any great popular movement. Historians were inclined to agree with him until Edward Thompson argued that the ideas of the Jacobin-Radicals had penetrated down the social scale and had been absorbed into the nascent working-class consciousness of early industrial England. The exclusion of the working classes from the reformed franchise in 1832 completed their 'making' as a separate class, conscious of itself. Henceforward, a political working-class movement was possible: Chartism was born, not in 1838 but in 1832. The key to Thompson's interpretation lies in his belief in the indivisible nature of human experience. Economic and political attitudes are inseparable, so the admittedly important economic dimension cannot be understood apart from the political. The contention of the radicals was that the economic grievances of the people had political causes and therefore needed political solutions. This had been argued by William Cobbett and other radical journalists after 1815, and the process of politicisation had been reinforced by the widespread debate, encouraged by middle-class propagandists, during the reform crisis of 1832.

Radicalism had been the traditional language of the excluded since the eighteenth century, but with the passage of the Reform Act in 1832 the lines of exclusion were redrawn, no longer between 'Old Corruption' and the 'People' but between the propertied and the unpropertied. Radicalism therefore became in effect the language of an excluded class. Hence legislation carried subsequently by the reformed parliament in the 1830s, contrary to the interests of the excluded, was termed 'class legislation' by the radicals. In particular it seemed that the newly-enfranchised middle classes were now able to influence legislation to advance their own interests. The logical conclusion was that only an enfranchised working class would be likely to legislate in its best interests – repealing the Poor Law Amendment Act, passing a Ten Hours Act, and securing a genuine repeal of the Corn Laws which would reduce prices without reducing wages. Until such a democratic parliament was elected, trade unionists would continue to be transported (for example, the Tolpuddle labourers in 1834, and Glasgow cotton spinners in 1837), and civil liberties would be denied as they had been to the Irish in 1833. In this way the social, economic and political grievances of the 1830s were subsumed within a broadly-based national movement to establish a democratic franchise [Thompson (9)].

LEADERSHIP AND ORGANISATION

In the early history of Chartism the central place afforded to the London Working Men's Association and the Birmingham Political Union is now being questioned. Instead, the London Working Men's Association is criticised for restricting the growth of Chartism in London by a policy of exclusiveness which was damaging to the development of a mass strategy in the capital. Far from having usurped the leadership of the nascent movement, O'Connor is seen to have played a major role in creating it through his lecture tours in 1835, his Great Northern Union of 1838, and the leading part he played in making the *Northern Star* newspaper the voice of Chartism across the country [Epstein (6)].

O'Connor came to English radicalism as a successor to Henry Hunt and William Cobbett, both of whom died in 1835, and his technique was that of the 'Platform' which Hunt had perfected [Belchem in (7)]. That is, Chartism was organised through mass meetings, the function of which was to inform, to demonstrate and to intimidate. The Petition was more of a middle-class idea, successfully used in the anti-slavery campaign and it was adopted with some initial misgivings by many Chartists. Another traditional device was the convention or anti-parliament, hallowed by its usage in 1689 and by the Americans in their struggle for independence. These three aspects of radical organisation were brought together in Chartism, with the mass meetings of 1838 and 1839 being called to elect delegates to the Convention and then to rally support for the Petition. The failure of this activity to produce the required effect led to important developments in renewed Chartist organisation which have until recently been neglected.

The foundation of the National Charter Association in July 1840 is seen as the turning point [Jones (4)]. This gave Chartism a leadership, at both national and local levels, in which working men played a more prominent part than in the early years of the movement, and which sustained Chartism for the next decade. Studies of Chartist 'localities' have drawn attention to the ways in which continuity was maintained between the peak years of mass petitioning. The local Chartist hall offered its members the opportunity to order their own leisure hours in accordance with the principles of the Charter, through educational and religious activities, entertainments and democratic participation by the whole family. And where there was no hall, there was often a reading group, meeting on Sundays to share in a communal copy of the *Northern Star* [Epstein and Yeo in (7)].

Indeed, the *Northern Star* is now regarded as probably the most important element in the Chartist organisation. Far from being O'Connor's mouthpiece, it gave voice to the whole movement, reporting activities in obscure corners of the land, conveying the content of major speeches by national figures in a style intended for reading out aloud and providing a public forum for the discussion of policy. Additionally, the *Star* was sufficiently profitable to fund the wider movement, enabling O'Connor to employ local reporters (often from among the unemployed or victimised) who could then in effect provide a semi-professional local leadership. Undoubtedly the paper did serve to keep O'Connor prominent in the movement, and ultimately his policies prevailed, but he tolerated considerable independence among his editors [Epstein (6)].

The new picture of O'Connor which emerges is a more sympathetic one than that presented by most of his contemporaries. Through his oratory and his place on the NCA executive, and as proprietor of the *Northern Star*, he provided the Chartists with the leadership which the rank and file wanted, whatever the rival leaders may have thought. He was a demagogue in the true sense of the word – he spoke for the people and remained popular because he articulated the aspirations of the inarticulate. Nowhere was this more true than with the Land Plan.

THE LAND PLAN

The Land Plan has usually been seen as conclusive evidence of O'Connor's inconsistent and misguided policies. This was the issue on which he quarrelled with several other leaders who felt either that the plan was not socialist enough or that it detracted from the radical political message that no social change could be effected without the Charter. Fellow Chartists who had been castigated for supporting the 'New Moves' – that is Church, Temperance or Education Chartism – now witnessed the biggest diversionary move of all. The Land Plan seemed to be turning English workers into Irish peasants; this was the work of Feargus O'Connor, more Irishman than Chartist.

It is true that O'Connor was influenced by his uncle Arthur O'Connor's pamphlet, *The State of Ireland*, which he republished in 1843, but his ideas on the land also had roots in British radical thinking. Thomas Spence's exposition of the Biblical teaching on 'Jubilee' (Leviticus 25, v. 10), when the land would be returned to its rightful owner, had become an integral part of radical ideology [Chase (12)]. The land was central to nineteenth-century radicals – readers of Cobbett, Owenites, O'Brienites, members of countless emigration societies and, later, the followers of Henry George. For

O'Connor to make an issue of the land within Chartism was nothing unusual. The appeal of the Land Company to thousands of labourers in town and country is therefore not surprising. What the land offered was independence from capitalists and middlemen; it gave direct access to employment and the means of subsistence; it restored control over life and the environment. Resettlement on the land also reduced the urban labour market and so benefited people everywhere. And at a time when the intransigence of Parliament was undermining the effectiveness of other forms of Chartist organisation, the Land Company held the mass membership together. O'Connor's financial mismanagement might therefore seem all the more culpable, were it not for the primitive state of the law on joint-stock holding, friendly societies and co-operatives which inhibited working-class organisations until the reforms of the 1850s [Yeo in (7)].

RANK AND FILE

O'Connor apart, the emphasis in recent scholarship has been more upon the led than the leaders among Chartism – or, at least, the lesser leaders, for that is all the evidence permits. What Chartism meant to them, and indeed who they were, has become central to the quest for a full understanding of the movement in all its diversity. Historians have concluded that most Chartists were ordinary people – that is they were by occupation, age and marital status typical of the communities in which they lived. This evidence also supports the contention that ordinary Chartists were capable of serious political thought: destitute weavers who were self-educated, widely-read and yearned for rights as well as bread. And although there were more men than women, the part played by women was not insignificant, particularly in the early years of the movement. Women were organised in their own radical societies and often provided their own speakers; they attended demonstrations and were to the forefront in riots such as occurred in the summer of 1842. Paradoxically, as Chartist organisation became more sophisticated their role was diminished to that of auxiliaries [Thompson (9)].

The Chartists had won their mass support by convincing those with social and economic discontents of their need for the radical panacea. The repeated failure of the political strategy undoubtedly did much to discredit those who argued that only by first winning political reform could they fulfil their other hopes. Moreover, the Chartist message was shown by events to be not only ineffective but untrue. Reforms did begin to come from that parliament of which it was claimed no good could come. The 'class legislation' of the 1830s was replaced in the 1840s by more neutral reforms [Stedman Jones in (7)]. O'Connor reconciled himself to Richard Cobden of the Anti-Corn Law League in 1844, and in 1846 the *Northern Star* hailed Peel's conversion to Corn Law repeal and support for agricultural improvements as a vindication of the Land Scheme and as a statesmanlike measure. The Ten Hours Act was secured in 1847, following the earlier Mines Act of 1842. Even the hated Poor Law Commission was dismantled in 1847 and, though the Act itself remained, it was not at this time implemented with the rigour which had been feared in the late 1830s. The apparent success of the Anti-Corn Law League was pointing the way forward for single-issue campaigns which might bring relief even without the Charter. Political reform was being demoted from the first essential reform to just one desired reform among many.

One problem with this view is that of timing. As a long-term explanation of the gradual erosion of support for Chartism it is persuasive, but mass support in the country at large began to fall away from 1839, and collapsed in many places after 1842, leaving only a rump of dedicated radicals in their Chartist localities. A more credible short-term explanation of failure remains disillusionment and exhaustion after such great promises and high hopes, together with the upswing in the economy from the summer of 1842.

Recent work on London has also challenged the view that Chartism was declining everywhere after 1842 [Goodway (8)]. The view that trade unionists stayed aloof from Chartism can no longer be sustained at the local and personal level. In London, Chartism was growing between 1839 and 1842, and remained strong in the trade societies of the metropolis until 1848 when the capital was the greatest centre of Chartist support. However, Dorothy Thompson has argued that Chartism could not have survived in the great cities of the later nineteenth century where working-class communities could be isolated, divided and controlled by police, schoolmasters and clergy. As a movement Chartism belonged to the smaller communities of provincial Britain, where working people shared the experiences of neighbourliness and neighbourhood. As social contexts changed, so different forms of working-class organisation emerged to replace the old-style mass politics of the platform. Struggles became centred on the place of work, trade unions offering defences for new skills as the old trades died out [Thompson (9)].

Changing perceptions of the state and shifting social and economic contexts help one understand why Chartism did not revive for a fourth time in the 1850s, but not why it did revive in 1848. This latter may at least in part be accounted for by the often underestimated strength of Chartist support, leadership and local organisation after 1842. Chartist failure in 1848 therefore cannot be explained simply in terms of Chartist weakness, and so historians have turned their attention to the corresponding strengths of the state. Unlike regimes on the Continent, that in Britain was securely based on a relatively broad property franchise and upheld by the consensus of the political nation. This was the intended result of the 1832 Reform Act which isolated the radicals. Moreover, the forces sustaining law and order were small but effective. London was well policed by 1839, and constables could be despatched to the provinces by train when necessary – for example, to Birmingham during the Bull Ring riots. The army was professional, well trained and competently led. Attempts to subvert the loyalty of the troops met with little success. Informers kept ministers aware of the more dangerous plans of revolutionary conspirators. When it needed to the government could strike swiftly at its opponents – picking off leaders with mass arrests in 1839, 1842 and 1848, then letting most of them go when tension had eased but convicting key figures to short periods in prison.

The strength of the government was most apparent in 1848.

NOT SO VERY UNREASONABLE!!! EH?"

John "My Mistress says she hopes you won't call a meeting of her Creditors: but if you will leave your Bill in the usual way, if shall be properly attended to."

Illustration 8   An initially favourable view of the Charter, 1848

THE CHARTIST PROCESSION ACCORDING TO THE SIGNATURES OF THE PETITION.

Illustration 9   A later mocking interpretation of the Charter, 1848

167

The myth of the 'fiasco' of 10 April (when there was a mass demonstration on Kennington Common and the presentation of the third petition), is no longer accepted. What that day entailed was not folly and cowardice by Chartists, but an enormous propaganda victory for the government in a situation which it did much to create in order to sustain its image both at home and abroad. The extent of that victory is suggested by *Punch*. Illustration 8 shows that the immediate response of *Punch* to the Petition of 1848 was not hostile. (The little doorman is the Prime Minister, Lord Russell.) The publication date of this cartoon is 15 April but that means it was printed before the revelations of 13 April about the false signatures on the Petition and before the tide of ridicule was in full flow. By contrast, two weeks later the Petition was thoroughly discredited and *Punch* joined in the mockery in its issue of 29 April, shown in Illustration 9. Far from the Chartists being discredited and disillusioned, they rallied and caused further problems in June, July and August which the government dealt with severely and in a less flamboyant manner [Saville (11)].

One argument, often rehearsed, is that failure was inevitable; the Chartists lacked unity in action, sufficient economic and political power to force a peaceful change, and the will to use force. Though this is probably true, it is unhistorical not to look for possible alternative outcomes. The language of physical force was frequently used, but historians have usually dismissed this as a tactic of bluff, or the raving of an isolated and untypical few. A re-examination of the Newport Rising has caused this line to be rethought, for we now know that the South Wales rising of November 1839 was a genuine attempt at revolution, widely supported in the Valleys and carefully planned over many months [Jones (10)]. Its failure was the outcome of bad weather, poor tactics and ill-luck – but it was a close-run thing. Other conspiracies in Yorkshire were less well organised, but could have been more threatening had the authorities suffered a severe defeat in South Wales. In 1839 the Chartist threat was very real in the provinces; the weakness of London at this date is therefore crucial in the failure of the Chartists to exert effective pressure for change at their time of maximum support in the country at large.

CONCLUSIONS

The picture of Chartism to emerge from recent writings is very different from that which prevailed earlier in this century. The economic interpretation is no longer regarded as adequate; there is a far greater appreciation of the political dimension to the Chartist movement. The focus of attention has moved from leaders to followers, from Chartism to the Chartists. O'Connor has been rehabilitated as the link between the two. Place and Lovett no longer dominate the historiography; more scholars read the *Northern Star* and mine its wealth of local detail. This is not to say, though, that the conclusions now reached are final or that they have been made in an ideological vacuum. Much of the recent work has been done by scholars wth an inclination towards the 'left'; historians with different perspectives still find much that is convincing in Disraeli's analysis of 1839. The debate is by no means concluded.

REFERENCES AND FURTHER READING

(1) **A. Briggs** (ed.), *Chartist Studies* (London, 1959).
(2) **J. T. Ward,** *Chartism* (London, 1973).
(3) **D. Thompson,** *The Early Chartists* (London, 1971).
(4) **D. Jones,** *Chartism and the Chartists* (London, 1975).
(5) **E. Royle,** *Chartism* (London, 1986).
(6) **J. Epstein,** *The Lion of Freedom. Feargus O'Connor and the Chartist Movement, 1832–1842* (London, 1982).
(7) **J. Epstein and D. Thompson** (eds), *The Chartist Experience. Studies in Working-Class Radicalism and Culture, 1830–1860* (London, 1982).
(8) **D. Goodway,** *London Chartism* (Cambridge, 1984).
(9) **D. Thompson,** *The Chartists* (London, 1984).
(10) **D. Jones,** *The Last Rising. The Newport Insurrection of 1839* (Oxford, 1985).
(11) **J. Saville,** *The British State and the Chartist Movement* (Cambridge, 1987).
(12) **M. Chase,** *The People's Farm. English Agrarian Radicalism, 1775–1840* (Oxford, 1987).

13 The Labour Aristocracy in the British Class Structure

R. J. Morris

In those days, the stonemasons, like the miners, were the aristocrats of labour. On the occasion of the marriage of my father and mother, they were driven to church in a four in hand with a postillion rider in front. As a symbol of affluence, my father wore a suit of white moleskins, whilst my mother wore a brand new Paisley shawl. The wedding supper was held in the public hall to which special invitations were issued to a large circle of friends. (Tom Bell, *Pioneering Days*, London 1941, p. 14)

The labour aristocracy were a section of the nineteenth-century working class who were relatively better paid, more secure, better treated at work and more able to control the organisation of their work. They had a distinctive 'respectable' life style. Contemporaries and historians used and use this concept to help to describe the inequalities of wealth and power in nineteenth-century industrial society. They used the term to help them account for change over time in that wider set of relationships called social class. The concept was important for several reasons. It drew attention to the complexity, inequality and differences *within* the British working class. This privileged stratum played an important part in explaining the social peace of the 1850s and 1860s which followed the violent and fundamental challenges to authority in the previous fifty years, the challenges of Painite radicalism, Owenism, violent and illegal trade unionism and Chartism. These accounts suggest that skilled workers benefited from the economic prosperity which free trade and the domination of world trade brought to the British economy. These benefits encouraged skilled workers to accept capitalist relationships and to restrict their political efforts to securing limited gains within the existing social and economic system. Thus the Owenite producer co-operatives of the 1830s were succeeded by retail co-operative stores which accepted the logic of the market system and distributed their profits to customer members. The old Chartists lost their independence in the new Liberal Party, amalgamated under Gladstone with the urban middle class and aristocratic Whigs. Both trade unions and employers alike sought to replace conflict with arbitration and conciliation involving unions operating within the law.

CLASS COLLABORATION?

Bargaining strength and bribery were emphasised by different accounts of this change [1]. Engels, who was one of the first to write about this issue, felt that the privileges of the skilled men were due to their superior bargaining power. He recognised that these benefits had to be defended by conflict but concluded that the result was to divide the wage-earning classes in a way which diverted them from the revolutionary role which he and Marx had envisaged at mid century. Lenin, on the other hand, believed that the employers and owners of capital had used the super-profits gained from the imperialist domination of world markets to bribe their own workers and thus ensure an alliance between the owners of capital and the labour aristocracy against, first the less skilled, and then against other countries. Early twentieth-century socialists saw the labour aristocracy as a skilled group 'isolated ... from the mass of the proletariat in close, selfish, craft unions' (Harry Quelch, 1913). These bribes and alliances ultimately helped socialists explain why the working people of Europe went to war against each other in 1914 in support of the imperial and industrial power of their leaders. The labour aristocracy has not been the exclusive property of Marxist and socialist writers. It has been closely associated with a pattern of behaviour called 'respectability' which was central to class, workplace, family and gender relationships.

171

In 1954, Eric Hobsbawm [2] outlined six factors which helped to identify a labour aristocracy, the level and regularity of a worker's earnings, their degree of social security, the nature and degree of their control of the work process, their relationships with other social classes, their general standard of living and the prospects of social advancement for themselves and their families. By the 1860s, just over 10 per cent of the British labour force earned over 28s. (£1.40) a week. This 10 per cent was almost without exception composed of adult males. They included rapidly growing groups of skilled wage labour like the engineers, shipwrights and iron puddlers. They included older trades like printers, glass bottle-makers and coachmakers. They included parts of trades like tailoring and bootmaking in which an aristocracy of labour survived by specialising in skilled high-quality work. Other groups had a more debatable place in this elite, such as coal hewers, adult male spinners, masons and other building trades. The labour aristocracy played an increasingly important part as a social and economic group after mid century because during the decades surrounding 1850, wage labour dominated more and more of the relationships between labour and capital, steadily replacing sub-contracting, independent craftsmen, domestic production and the workshop production of small masters. Fewer skilled men could look forward to a natural lifetime progression from apprentice, to journeyman, to master. They now looked to trade unions like the Associated Society of Engineers to defend their prosperity.

This picture of class collaboration, whether brought about by bribery or bargaining strength, was considerably elaborated by three major case studies made during the 1970s.

BRIBERY AND CULTURAL ASSAULT BY EMPLOYERS

In a detailed study of the cotton spinning and engineering town of Oldham between the 1790s and 1860s, John Foster identified a powerful working-class revolutionary movement which in the late 1830s and the 1840s came to dominate key elements of local government through exclusive dealing and an alliance with radical members of the middle classes [3].

Poor law and police policy and the choice of parliamentary representatives were used in ways which challenged the dominant ideology of employer authority within a profit-seeking cash economy. The economic and authority structure of industrial society was challenged not only by violent trade union action but by sustained ideological criticism. The potential of this working-class power was dissipated in the 1850s by a process he called 'liberalisation'. He set out to demonstrate that 'Oldham's bourgeoisie consciously used its industrial power (and the economic and psychological reality of empire) to split the labour force and bribe its upper layers into political acquiescence' [(3) p. 204].

There were two major elements in this process. First, the labour force in three leading industries was restructured in a way which produced a privileged section which in turn helped sustain the authority of the employers. After the defeat of the engineers' strike in 1852, the craft autonomy of the engineers was replaced by a piecemaster system, within which a larger part of the simpler preparatory work was done by boys under eighteen. In cotton spinning the adult måle spinner was transformed into a pacemaker. There was no clear split in the coal industry, although the introduction of the checkweighman and the sliding scale agreements in the 1860s suggested a reduction in the direct conflict between labour and employer.

The second element in the change was a massive assault upon the cultural institutions of working people. Sunday schools emphasised religious rather than secular education, the friendly societies were increasingly brought under state control through the Registrar General of Friendly Societies, the magistrates used the licensing system to control the public house, the working-class meeting place, and a wide range of middle-class-sponsored cultural agencies, such as mechanics' institutions, were offered to working people. These cultural agencies all emphasised the virtues of the work ethic, savings, education, and religion within the market economy. Broader issues arising from this aspect of the debate are discussed by Michael Thompson in Chapter 14.

173

Subsequent work has modified much of this. Studies of places like Preston, where the size of factories was much larger than Oldham, have shown that the industrial trade unions of the cotton spinners played a major part in institutionalising conflict. The increased willingness of many employers to work with the trade unions did not prevent often bitter and prolonged strikes but it did provide a framework within which conflict was limited and, equally important, detached from politics. Secondly, an important study of Blackburn and other Lancashire mill towns [4] showed that authority at work in the cotton mills was identified not with an isolated stratum of the working class but with age and gender. This hierarchy was linked to the values of the 'respectable working class' and their lifetime expectations of moving from doffer to piecer to spinner, or in the case of women through the weaving shed to marriage. Assumptions about the authority of men over women, of adults over teenagers, were used to support the authority of the employers. Lastly it was clear that the Lancashire mill owners approached labour as a whole, re-creating a structure of paternalism within the mill communities as industrial technology stabilised in the 1850s. The link between owner and labour was reinforced by political identities like Gladstonian Liberalism and Orange Toryism. The link was reinforced by small doles, tied cottages, the provision of community resources such as parks and adult education and above all by factory celebrations of the life-cycle events of the owner's own family. This section of the literature showed clearly that the development of a labour aristocracy as an isolated stratum of the working class was not the only source of the increasing stability of class relationships after 1850.

A WELL-PAID ELITE

Two studies of Edinburgh and of 'Kentish' London examined communities where the existence of an upper stratum of the working class was much clearer. The years 1850–80 saw the creation of an élite of relatively well-paid and secure skilled men employed in the engineering, shipbuilding, munitions and building industries of Greenwich, Deptford and Woolwich [5]. In Edinburgh the level and regularity of the earnings of printers, engineers, masons and even shoemakers stood above those of the unskilled labourers. The Edinburgh evidence showed that this had clear results in terms of the rent paid for housing, the number from each occupation who ended up in the poorhouse, and even the heights of their children [6].

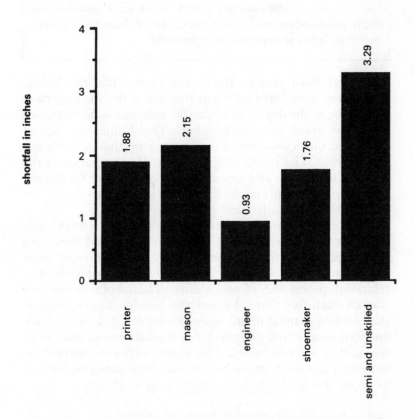

Figure 9 Height of children as shortfall from the average at Broughton School in Edinburgh 1904

Source: Based on figures in Grey [6], p. 97

175

The heights of the children reflected long-term contrasts in the standard of living of their families. They were measured in 1904 by the Charity Organisation Society and expressed in terms of their shortfall compared to the height of all children of their age at Broughton School, which served the families of shopkeepers and clerks as well as the artisans (see box) and

---

The term **artisan** in this article has the usage which developed in the first half of the nineteenth century. It refers to skilled manual labour in trades which had or had just lost that independence which went with small workshop production and the possibility of lifetime upward mobility from **journeyman** to **master**.

---

labourers. Both studies tested the claim that the labour aristocracy were 'isolated' from the rest of the working class by looking at the degree to which the different socio-economic groups married with each other. The Edinburgh figures compared the occupation of the groom with that of the father of the bride. The London figures took the occupation of the father of both bride and groom (given the evidence for lifetime upward mobility this might have been expected to reduce the overlap between skilled and unskilled).

The results showed several features of the British class structure (see figures 10 and 11). Skilled men and their sons were much more likely to marry into the families of other skilled men than into the families of the unskilled. The relationship was one of probability. The labour aristocracy was no exclusive caste. Indeed the London figures suggest that the non-manual middle classes were more likely to marry amongst themselves (despite being a small group) than were the skilled working class. The status divisions within the working class were important for marriage patterns, but not as important as the division between social classes.

CULTURAL AND ECONOMIC INDEPENDENCE

Both these studies found cultural evidence which suggested that the notion of 'collaboration' between the labour aristocracy

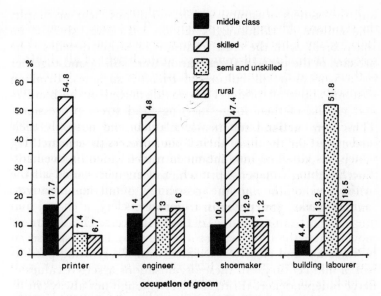

Figure 10 Distribution of fathers-in-law in Edinburgh, 1865–9
Source: Based on figures in Gray [6], p.112.

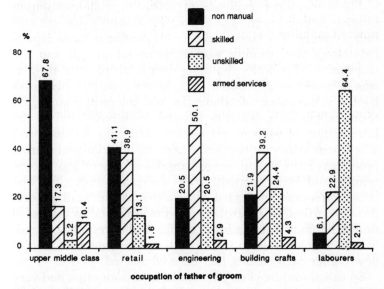

Figure 11 Distribution of the occupation of fathers-in-law in Kentish London, 1851–75

and the owners of capital was by no means clear or simple. The culture of Edinburgh's labour aristocracy showed no sharp break with the craft traditions of earlier decades. The artisans of the post-1850 generation were still bound together by a workshop sub-culture of friendly societies, drinking customs and craft pride. This was displayed in the banners and regalia of their lodge meetings and street processions. These spectacular banners which celebrated not only their leaders but the details of their labour process were something which has survived into the modern trade union movement. The Edinburgh masons, printers and engineers used all the institutions of the labour aristocracy, retail co-operatives, savings banks, and perhaps a literary society, a chapel and one of the artisan companies of the Volunteers. The Volunteer movement of the 1860s was a sort of territorial army sponsored by the state and closely associated with the growing patriotism of mid century. All these organisations asserted values of fierce independence, thrift, sobriety (though not always in its extreme form, teetotalism), orderly conduct and a rigid family morality.

There was little evidence of bribes or collaboration in London or Edinburgh. The artisan's dominant value was still independence. The labour aristocrat's dominant social experience, from the printing workshops of Edinburgh and the shipyards of London to building sites in all parts of Britain, was of persistent attempts by employers to reduce privileges by the sub-division of labour, by technological change, by hiring labour on a casual or job-and-finish basis, and by the introduction of women and boys to dilute the labour force. The labour aristocrat survived where organisation and market power gave strength in wage-bargaining. There was a continuing and bitter struggle over workplace authority. The labour aristocrat defended his control of the work process through strikes, by control of apprenticeship and by control of time discipline. For the ironmoulder in the west of Scotland, 'it was a union rule to take a rest of fifteen minutes to cool down' after each casting had been completed.

So-called middle-class patterns of behaviour often had very different meanings when practised by these skilled men. Education helped the artisan keep up with technological change, especially important for the printers. Savings meant that the artisan could resist pressures for downgrading during times of sickness or trade depression. More important, savings made wage-earners a more formidable strike threat during wage-bargaining. The labour aristocracy plundered middle-class culture for products to mould into their own traditions. Values of respectability and self-help brought a congruence and sympathy between the views and behaviour of large sections of middle and skilled working class. These values were self-generated. The 'independent' nature of the skilled man's politics meant that the social stability achieved by the congruence of middle-class and skilled working-class cultures contained within it the sources of its own instability. This showed very clearly in Kentish London where the artisans marched cheerfully into the Gladstonian Liberal Party of the 1860s but this party then failed to deliver radical measures and failed to admit these politically aware artisans to decision-making positions in local parties. Expectations raised by the sympathy of values were disappointed. These disappointed expectations were one element in the very different contribution which these same labour aristocratic skilled men made to political, social and economic relationships in the early twentieth century.

CHANGING POLITICAL VALUES

This instability emerged clearly between 1880 and 1920. By the 1890s, the economic and technological conditions which had created the labour aristocracy were changing, notably for the engineers [7]. New semi-automatic machinery threatened their ability to control the labour process. New methods of management, called 'Taylorism' after its American origins, with its time and motion studies and resulting speed ups, together with an increased sub-division of labour were equally threatening. The ASE (Associated Society of Engineers) saw the main purpose of the turret lathe, the universal drilling machine and the grinding machine as the reduction of 'the number of highly skilled men, that is the fitters'. These and similar changes in other trades threatened the moral economy

179

of the skilled man, especially his ability to earn a 'family wage'. The family wage enabled the skilled man to keep his wife at home, creating that clean, neat and comfortable house which he prized so much. It enabled him to put his sons to apprenticeships and his daughters into respectable jobs instead of forcing them out to work at an early age to counter family poverty. As these pressures grew a small number of these men emerged from their advanced liberal politics, democratic, fiercely moralistic and often internationalist, and joined one of the fragments which were to become the Labour Party of 1918.

The potential for bitter conflict contained in the so-called collaborationist values of the labour aristocracy reached a peak in 1915 during the Glasgow rent strike. Wartime inflation forced up rents well beyond the levels which rapidly rising wages could meet. Hardest hit were the 'soldiers' wives' several of whom were involved in evictions which ran counter to that mixture of family values, patriotism and sense of justice which the skilled families inherited from their parents. Women were the initial leaders in the strike because their traditional role included the management of household spending. They rapidly gained support from the engineering shop stewards who already saw 'dilution' of labour by women and unskilled boys as a threat to that economic power which had brought a rent-paying 'family wage' in the first place. The government of the day solved the immediate crisis with a Rent Act which destroyed the ability of the economy to supply low-income housing through the free market. This was the first and one of the most significant results of the manner in which the skilled men were questioning the free market upon which their mid-century prestige had been based. These same skilled men, together with wives and daughters who joined the Women's Co-operative Guild and the Independent Labour Party, became a key element in the leadership and membership of the new Labour Party. Their values and experience were to play a major part in the subsequent history of that party.

CONCLUSIONS

Historians have gathered growing evidence that the values of the labour aristocracy were self-generated from earlier craft and artisan traditions. They selected from and reinterpreted the cultural products offered them by higher social classes. The economic advantages which made possible their respectable, family wage lifestyle were won and defended by bargaining strength. The congruence of labour aristocrat and middle-class values did make it easier to negotiate many of the conflicts inherent in the relationships of wage labour during the 1850s and 1860s, but the expectations raised by that congruence contained elements of later conflict and challenge to dominant authority within British industrial society. Thus the nature and experience of a labour aristocracy contributed to class and political relationships in twentieth-century Britain.

REFERENCES AND FURTHER READING

(1) **John Field,** 'British Historians and the Concept of the Labour Aristocracy', *Radical History Review,* 19 (Winter 1978–9).
(2) **E. J. Hobsbawm,** 'The Labour Aristocracy in Nineteenth Century Britain, and Trends in the British Labour Movement', in *Labouring Men* (London, 1964).
(3) **John Foster,** *Class Struggle and the Industrial Revolution. Early Industrialism in three English Towns* (London, 1974).
(4) **Patrick Joyce,** *Work, Society and Politics. The culture of the factory in later Victorian England* (Brighton, 1980).
(5) **Geoffrey Crossick,** *An Artisan Elite in Victorian Society. Kentish London 1840–1880* (London, 1978).
(6) **Robert Gray,** *The Labour Aristocracy in Victorian Edinburgh* (Oxford, 1976).
(7) **R. J. Morris,** 'Skilled Workers and the Politics of the "Red" Clyde', *Journal of Scottish Labour History,* no. 18 (1983).

14 Social Control in Modern Britain

F. M. L. THOMPSON

All good history, which is to say lively, interesting, and intellectually challenging history, borrows concepts from other disciplines. These instruments for the dissection and interpretation of the past may come from law, theology, economics, politics, psychology, anthropology, and many other sources. Without them history is a simple chronicle of events; and it could be said that the narrative historian in order to be good needs to acquire the skills of the storyteller. The appearance of the term 'social control' in the vocabulary of social historians, a concept developed by sociologists and anthropologists, is thus part of a long-standing and continuing process which is continually broadening and deepening the field, and the texture, of historical writing. The trouble is that while tools used by the historical demographer, such as 'gross reproduction rate', or the economic historian, such as 'net national income per capita', have precise technical meanings which give them a clear cutting edge, encouraging them to be used with care, equipment taken from the sociologist's tool-bag tends to look homely, familiar, and harmless, encouraging a certain amount of unreflecting and unskilled use for inappropriate jobs. Thus 'social control' is at once a phrase which appears to have a plain, commonsense, uncomplicated meaning – that those in power and authority are always trying to control the rest of society in one way or another – and also a concept drawn from theoretical sociology. This ambiguity has spread confusion and incoherence in much recent writing on modern social history; while the fashionability of the new terminology has led some early modernists to introduce essentially superfluous and redundant verbiage into their work.

SOCIAL CONTROL AND SOCIALISATION

'The concept of social control' A. P. Donajgrodzki could write in 1977 when introducing a collection of essays on *Social Control in Nineteenth-Century Britain,* 'will be unfamiliar to many historians' [1]. Since then the phrase has become familiarised into textbooks, even though the concept itself may not have become any better understood.

The missionary zeal kindled by the discovery of a new philosopher's stone has inspired a school of thought which portrays the social order and its cultural and ideological underpinning as the product of ceaseless manipulations and refinements of mechanisms of social control. These are said to influence a whole array of social institutions and mechanisms, including churches, schools, music halls, or football matches. Besides the services which are their ostensible and explicit object – salvation, education, amusement, excitement – these institutions and mechanisms send coded messages which determine the morals, standards, values, and general patterns of behaviour of the people. They do so by infiltrating the desired norms into those parts of their lives which are spent as worshippers, students, audiences, or spectators. It might seem to be a truism that any social institution at any period in history and in any type of society, be it feudal, capitalist, communist, authoritarian, fascist, democratic, Christian, Moslem, Hindu, or Hottentot, necessarily has rules, codes of conduct, and accepted ways of behaving with which its members are constrained to conform by a variety of moral and physical sanctions. Not even a family can exist as a social unit without some structure of accepted relationships between its members and some agreement on their understood roles, whether achieved by affection, calculation, or compulsion. Indeed, in some senses the family is the basic cell in the machinery of social control, the institution which socialises (or when broken, or defective, fails to socialise) children into the manners and mores of the segment of society which they inhabit.

This implies that the mechanisms of social control may have profoundly traditional, conservative, and conformist purposes, being designed to sustain and reproduce the beliefs

183

and behaviour which the controlling authority (parent, teacher, priest) deems to be acceptable and normal. It is therefore unsurprising that the concept originated (well over half a century before social historians got to hear of it) as part of a highly conservative sociology, designed to provide a theoretical basis for explaining how groups in the community cope with deviants, nonconformists, and rebels. At that stage in the discourse the terms 'socialisation' and 'social control' were interchangeable. Or, more precisely, the socialisation of individuals into an acceptable life style and conformity to acceptable standards of behaviour simply described the process, and condition, produced by the exercise of social control. This was wielded by those with authority as guardians of the group's rules and customs. In effect what was happening was the development of a specialised language to describe the mechanisms of social discipline. The language was made difficult and obscure, as is normally the case when specialist professionals invent a vocabulary for their subject. But it was useful in describing what might be called the social 'potty-training', or social conditioning, which is perpetually going on so that society can reproduce itself. The terms had descriptive but no explanatory power. They could not explain why great store was set upon the chastity of middle-class Victorian girls, why respectable working-class homes had holystoned doorsteps and unused front parlours, why skilled upholsterers in top hats were waited upon by apprentice boys, or why miners grew prize leeks instead of singing revolutionary songs. They could describe how such attitudes were transmitted and reproduced within an essentially static society.

HISTORICAL APPLICATIONS

History, however, is concerned with understanding the processes of change. It was natural, therefore, that when social historians began to incorporate these concepts into their own tool-kits they should redesign the tools to perform dynamic and explanatory tasks. The key step was to differentiate between 'socialisation' and 'social control' in a way which had not been originally intended. 'Socialisation' was reserved to

First, then, you were taught to come to school, with clean hands, face and hair; because dirt spoils and dishonours those comely bodies which God has given us, and makes them more liable to disease. Next, you were taught order, to put away your things, your hats or cloaks or bonnets, in their proper places, to be civil and respectful in your behaviour towards your teachers, and gentle to each other; to be silent during lessons; and to conform to all the other rules of your school. This was the first part of your education; and these things are taught first, not because they are important, but because they are necessary to the peace and comfort of others, and therefore to the order of the school ... It was necessary, then, that you should first learn to be civil, gentle, and orderly; for this is *part of your duty to your neighbour.*

Illustration 10 Priorities in elementary education. (An extract from the *Sequel to the Second book of lessons for the use of schools*, published in 1847 by the Commissioners on National Education in Ireland. These esteemed 'Irish school books' were widely used in elementary schools in mid-nineteenth-century Britain.)

refer to the processes by which a social group or association (family, church, chapel, public school, regiment, trade union) transmits its special imprint of values and customs from generation to generation, and especially to its new recruits. 'Social control' was uncoupled from this whole area of environmental conditioning. It was liberated for use in describing and analysing the processes by which groups with power and authority impose their value systems on the rest of society. This was normally by indirect cultural and ideological pressures rather than by brute force and direct decree. The social order, as one formulation has put it, 'is maintained not only, or even mainly by legal systems, police forces and prisons, but is expressed through a wide range of social institutions, from religion to family life, and including, for example, leisure and recreation, education, charity and philanthropy, social work and poor relief' [1]. Social control is thought of as one of the functions, although not as the sole purpose or motivation, of all these institutions.

The attractions of this approach for modern historians have been three-fold.

(i) Explanation

They are looking at the rise of an urban and industrial society from the middle of the eighteenth century onwards, and it appears that the social bonds and largely informal social institutions of 'traditional society' were breaking down under the pressures of population growth, urban concentration, and industrialisation. Successful manipulation of the levers of social control by the ruling class and the middle class seems to provide an explanation of how the working-class masses, after a few scaring episodes of disorder and insubordination like Peterloo and Chartism, were tamed and conditioned to accept their role at the bottom of the class structure of 'modern society'.

(ii) Integration

The notion that one of the aims of all manner of extremely diverse and heterogeneous voluntary associations and pressure groups was to influence and mould the character and behaviour of the poor or the masses provides a unifying and integrating framework for a welter of miscellaneous and disparate activities.

(iii) Context

Individual historians who are colonising new territories for social history and studying subjects like holidays, music halls, parks, pubs, or sport which have not seriously been investigated before, find valuable moral and intellectual support in drawing on the conceptual apparatus of social control to show how their particular research fits into the context of wider historical significance.

186

Social control theory has been fruitful in opening up the history of leisure, recreation and education. The social control thesis on popular leisure and recreation is supported by upper- and middle-class efforts at interference and regulation; attempts to substitute healthy, improving and disciplined pursuits for unsupervised, mindless, and disorderly debauchery. In popular education social control purposes were evident in the aim of the voluntary schools to impart codes of morality, religion, obedience, cleanliness, and discipline as an integral part of the method of teaching the three Rs. On inspection both of these turn out to be, in a broad sense, manifestations of the same social force: early-nineteenth-century evangelicalism. Evangelicals in the Anglican church and in the Dissenting chapels, especially among the Methodists, were deeply concerned about the irreligion, immorality, sinfulness, frivolity, ignorance, and mere pleasure-seeking of much of the society around them. They set out to remedy that state of affairs through their preaching and example, and through institutions like Sunday schools, voluntary schools, clubs, temperance halls, or charitable bodies, which would cultivate and implant virtuous habits. The ideal of a genuinely Christian population whose beliefs informed everyday actions and behaviour was all too easily diverted into the hypocrisies of middle-class Victorian ideas of propriety and respectability. Highly-principled disapproval of cruel sports, or of apparently unbridled drink and sex at traditional fairs, was readily confused with the sectional self-interest of groups of property-owners and residents anxious to suppress particular local nuisances. Nevertheless, there was an influential evangelically-inspired body of opinion.

This led to a campaign for rational recreation – meaning healthy, mind-improving, and orderly recreations like organised games, athletics, and gardening – and for popular education in schools managed on Christian principles and guided by religious beliefs in their teaching. The explicit aim was to bring about a reformation of morals and manners, to instil a new cultural order, and to instruct the lower orders on the duties and demeanour appropriate to their place in it. To

187

that extent the cultural purposes and methods of evangelicalism were those of social control. It would be a mistake,
however, to suppose that this was a class movement aimed at
subordinating the working class to bourgeois values under the
cloak of muscular Christianity. For one thing evangelicals had
loose-living, self-indulgent, gambling, and adulterous aristocrats in their sights, as well as rough, blasphemous and
ignorant sections of the working class. For another, evangelicalism cannot be described as the religious or ideological
instrument of middle-class interests. It was viewed with
detachment or distaste by probably the majority of practical
men of affairs and businessmen in the middle classes. And it
was adopted by a large minority of the working classes; chiefly
among the skilled and the miners, who saw self-improvement
and social dignity as the rewards for self-help, thrift, discipline,
godliness, and temperance.

It would be a greater mistake to imagine that working-class
adjustment to, and broad acceptance of, the forms of modern
capitalist society, which was apparent by the last quarter of
the nineteenth century, were due to the successful operation of
the social control devices which have been outlined. Religious
feelings and sectarian rivalry were certainly responsible for
the origins of the voluntary schools and their growth up to the
1870 Education Act, and they were carefully designed on class
lines to provide elementary education suited to the needs and
status of the lower classes, while superior education was
provided in separate schools – grammar, private, and public –
for the higher classes. Such features encourage belief in a
religious social control thesis. So too does the statement by Sir
James Graham, when introducing his abortive Education Bill
in 1843, in the midst of the Chartist disturbances. 'The police
and the soldiers have done their duty, the time is arrived when
moral and religious instructors must go forth to reclaim the
people from the errors of their ways.' These schools, however,
became markedly more secular and utilitarian in their emphasis, and less didactic, from the 1850s and particularly from
1862. In any case, attendance by an individual child was
likely to be so short, and so irregular, that the capacity of a
school to leave a permanent imprint on character, morals, or
beliefs was extremely limited.

Rational recreation, which set out to eliminate pubs, cruel sports, gambling, street games, and much else besides, was possibly even less successful. The public house was, and remained, the centre of much working-class culture. At the beginning of the nineteenth century the public house had a virtual monopoly as a meeting house for working people. The nineteenth-century attack on pubs as centres of an under-world of sex, indecency, depravity, crime, cock-fighting, gambling, and subversion was an expression of a traditional attitude. But it was a strikingly articulate expression, and one which was orchestrated by energetic evangelical and dissenting hands into the nationwide temperance movement. However, the overall impact of efforts aimed directly at curtailing the number and accessibility of beerhouses and pubs was rather limited. Most temperance reformers looked for better results from the provision of teetotal substitute meeting places and social centres which would lead the masses to a willing and joyful rejection of the demon drink. Clubs and societies for working men were launched with this end in view, under middle-class patronage. By the 1860s a whole network of working-men's clubs was coming into existence. No bourgeois lesson was required to teach working men the benefits and pleasures of association. A takeover of the works of middle-class benefactors and would-be social controllers ensued, in which working men assumed club management, and introduced the sale of beer. And the pub, as the centre of working-class culture, was stoutly defended, and survived into the age of canned beers and television without great difficulty.

Street games and street life more generally were suppressed, controlled, or swept into back alleys not by moral pressure but by police action. Some historians, indeed, have presented the new police forces and their social effects in the language of social control, and it is true that their discretionary powers to decide what constituted a 'nuisance' or an 'obstruction' were used to harass ordinary working-class people who were doing nothing that they had not always done and whose offence was to disregard unwritten and essentially middle-class rules about proper and improper conduct in public places. It is,

Illustration 11 Impressions of a London beershop. (From *The Drunkard's Children* (1848), by George Cruikshank, the most famous of the teetotal artists.)

Illustration 12 Temperance refreshment: the Coffee Room at Dorking. (This was organised in the 1870s by the temperance reformer, Lady Hope, as part of the coffee public house movement. Its advertisment read 'Coffee, tea, cocoa, or any other drink served EXCEPT beer, wine or spirits . . . No bad language allowed'.)

however, misleading and confusing to see the police as agents of social control; they are agents of government and their authority rests on the sanctions of the law and the coercive power of the state, not on the techniques of influence and persuasion. It is, of course, perfectly possible to argue that neither the law nor the police are necessarily objective, detached and socially neutral. They can be, and have been, used as instruments of class discrimination and oppression, as well as of religious, ethnic, or gender discrimination. But this is a separate issue, concerning the exercise of power and authority, and its attempted inclusion in the social control thesis makes that concept meaningless in its vagueness and generality.

Many popular recreations of the bull-running, cock-fighting, or village 'football' fight variety were indeed replaced in the course of the nineteenth century by more orderly and controlled diversions. But this was due less to the gospel of rational recreation than to the provision of counter-attractions through the commercialisation of leisure. Music halls, trips to the seaside, excursion trains, funfairs and fairgrounds, cycle tracks, and spectator sports, above all football, grew vigorously in the second half of the nineteenth century (especially in the last quarter), and were eagerly incorporated into popular culture. No doubt they had significant cultural effects, both as attractions which diverted working-class energies from pursuit of class conflict, and as activities which formalised the distinction between leisure time and work time. In so doing they reinforced the regularity and discipline of industrial work, which had been disrupted by older practices of casual absenteeism. It is also true that the entrepreneurs who provided these commercial entertainments had an interest in ensuring the orderly behaviour of their customers, for they had valuable plant and equipment to protect from damage. To risk courting police intervention and closure could be extremely bad for business. All the same, these were but the indirect behavioural consequences of commercial operations, of a kind which economic activities always produce. The leisure entrepreneurs supplied entertainment, amusement, fantasy, and illusion because it was profitable to meet a popular demand, that was generated by rising real incomes of

> *Sing a song of Saturday*
> *Wages taken home*
> *Ev'ry penny well laid out,*
> *None allowed to roam!* ...
>
> *Sing a song of Sunday,*
> *A home that's black and bare*
> *Wife and children starving,*
> *A crust of bread their share!* ...
>
> *Sing a song of Monday*
> *Brought before the 'beak'.*
> *Fine of twenty shillings,*
> *Alternative 'a week'!*
>
> *Workhouse for the children,*
> *Workhouse for the wife!*
> *Isn't that a hideous blot*
> *On our English life?*

From the commentary of a child's temperance picture book of the 1890s, which contrasted the weekend of a sober man with that of a drunkard.

Illustration 13 Teaching temperance

the working classes. To call the proprietor of a music hall, the owner of a steam roundabout, or the manager of a railway company, unconscious agents of social control is mere verbiage which tells us nothing about them which we did not know already from knowledge of their occupations and the nature of their businesses.

CONCLUSIONS

A critical appraisal of the social control approach leads to an alternative interpretation of that process of social transformation which led to a social order appropriate to an urban, industrial, capitalist society. It can be accepted that this social order was sustained not only by legal systems, police and prisons, but also by the non-coercive agencies discussed in this

193

chapter. However, it should be recognised both that there was often a yawning gap between the aims and achievements of such social controllers and that improvers and reformers were often socialisers rather than controllers. The great change in the social habits of the masses came about as a result of many convergent factors, material as well as attitudinal. Notable amongst them were: the discipline of factory work; the enforcement of law through more professional police; an improvement in living standards and, related to this, a process of emulation embodying a self-induced socialisation of ambition and aspiration. Most important in this reassessment is the renewed appreciation that working-class history had its own vitality and rationale; it was more than a derivative series of responses to middle-class educators and manipulators.

There is a truism lurking here: that economic relationships are also social relationships. The most powerful and direct influences over workers are exerted by employers, and over citizens by the state and its apparatus of laws and administration. The extent to which 'Victorian values' of self-help, thrift, hard work, independence, punctuality, sobriety, cleanliness, and respectability in general, were ever widely accepted can be doubted. But in so far as they did become part of working-class culture they derived from the work experience, the presence of the police, and the influence of the chapel. These influences may, if desired, be described as forms of social control. But it is more straightforward to say that employers manage and control workers, police control crowds, and ministers lead congregations. There is no separate and additional function which they perform beyond these, which can be labelled 'social control'. Social control as a theory for explaining class relationships dissolves when it is approached closely. What is left are a couple of words that act as a salutary reminder that all political, social, and economic institutions have some effects on types and standards of behaviour and contribute to the shaping of cultures or life styles.

REFERENCES AND FURTHER READING

(1) **A. P. Donajgrodzki** (ed.), *Social Control in Nineteenth-Century Britain* (Croom Helm, 1977).
(2) **G. Stedman Jones,** *Languages of Class* (Cambridge, 1983).
(3) **F. M. L. Thompson,** 'Social Control in Victorian Britain,' *Economic History Review*, 2nd ser. XXXIII (1981).
(4) **S. Cohen and A. Scull** (eds), *Social Control and the State. Historical and Comparative Essays* (Oxford, 1983).
(5) **R. Gray,** 'The Deconstruction of the English Working Class', *Social History*, 11 (1986).
(6) **P. Joyce,** 'In Pursuit of Class: Recent Studies in the History of Work and Class', *History Workshop Journal*, 25 (1988).
(7) **R. Price,** 'Conflict and Cooperation: a Reply to Patrick Joyce', *Social History*, 9 (1984).
(8) **J. Zeitlin,** 'Social Theory and the History of Work', *Social History*, 8 (1983).

195

Notes on Contributors

Nick Crafts is Professor of Economic History at the University of Warwick. He is the author of numerous papers on economic growth in Britain and Europe and of *British Economic Growth during the Industrial Revolution* (1985).

Tom Devine is Professor of Scottish History at the University of Strathclyde. Among his books on Scotland are *Lairds and Improvement in Enlightenment Scotland* (1979) and *The Great Highland Famine: Hunger, Emigration and the Scottish Highlands in the Nineteenth Century* (1988).

Anne Digby is currently Senior Lecturer in Social History at Oxford Polytechnic, and Research Associate at the Institute of Economics in the University of Oxford.

Charles Feinstein is Reader in Recent Economic and Social History at the University of Oxford, and Fellow of Nuffield College, Oxford.

Roderick Floud was formerly Professor of Modern History at Birkbeck College, University of London, and is now the Director of the City of London Polytechnic. His most recent book – written in collaboration with A. Gregory and K. W. Wachter – is *The Heights of the British, 1750–1980*, which will be published in 1989.

Sally Harvey has held lectureships in Medieval History at the universities at Leeds and Oxford. She has published several articles on the Domesday Inquiry, and *Domesday Book and its Purpose* in 1987.

Tony Hopkins is Professor of Economic History at the University of Birmingham. He is completing a book, written jointly with P. J. Cain, reinterpreting British imperialism in the nineteenth and twentieth centuries.

196

Jane Lewis is Reader in Social Science and Administration at the London School of Economics. She has written extensively on women and women's history, notably in *The Politics of Motherhood* (1980) and *Women in England 1870–1950* (1984).

Roger Middleton is Lecturer in Economic History at the University of Bristol. He is the author of a number of papers on British economic policy and of *Towards the Managed Economy: Keynes, the Treasury, and the Fiscal Policy Debate of the 1930s* (1985).

Bob Morris is Senior Lecturer in the Department of Economic and Social History at the University of Edinburgh. He has written *Class and Class Consciousness during the Industrial Revolution, 1790–1850* (1979), and was co-editor of *The Atlas of Industrializing Britain, 1790–1914* (1986).

Mark Overton is Lecturer in Geography at the University of Newcastle. The author of many articles on agrarian history, he is completing a monograph, *Agricultural Revolution in England: the transformation of the rural economy, 1550–1830*.

Ted Royle is Senior Lecturer in History at the University of York. Notable amongst his many publications in Social History are *Radicals, Secularists, and Republicans* (1980), and *Modern Britain. A Social History, 1750–1985* (1987).

Pat Thane is a Senior Lecturer in the Department of Social Science and Administration at Goldsmith's College in the University of London. A specialist in the recent history of social policy, she has written extensively on welfare provision, including *The Foundations of the Welfare State* (1982).

Michael Thompson is Director of the Institute of Historical Research in the University of London. Among his many publications on economic and social history are *English Landed Society in the Nineteenth Century* (1963) and *The Rise of Respectable Society. A Social History of Victorian Britain* (1988).

197

Michael Turner is Senior Lecturer in Economic History at the University of Hull. Among his publications are *English Parliamentary Enclosure* (1980) and *Enclosures in Britain 1750–1830* (1984).

Tony Wrigley was formerly Professor of Population Studies at the London School of Economics, and Director of the ESRC Cambridge Group for the History of Population and Social Structure, and is now a Senior Research Fellow at All Souls College, Oxford. He is the co-author of *The Population History of England 1541–1871. A Reconstruction* (1981).

Index

199

200

201

202